THE HAPPY
PLACE

THE HAPPY PLACE

A read-and-journal book to help you find and stay in your chosen happy place

2ND Edition

NANCY MILTON CPCC, ACC

Certified Coach and Life Skills Speaker

iUniverse, Inc.
Bloomington

The Happy Place
A read-and-journal book to help you find and stay in your chosen happy place

Second Edition
Copyright © 2012 by Nancy Milton CPCC, ACC.
Edits and Support by Jennifer Gourley
Cover Illustrations: iUniverse
Cover Design: Nancy Milton

iUniverse books may be ordered through booksellers or by contacting:

iUniverse
1663 Liberty Drive
Bloomington, IN 47403
www.iuniverse.com
1-800-Authors (1-800-288-4677)

Because of the dynamic nature of the Internet, any web addresses or links contained in this book may have changed since publication and may no longer be valid. The views expressed in this work are solely those of the author and do not necessarily reflect the views of the publisher, and the publisher hereby disclaims any responsibility for them.

Any people depicted in stock imagery provided by Thinkstock are models, and such images are being used for illustrative purposes only.
Certain stock imagery © Thinkstock.

ISBN: 978-1-4697-9171-5 (sc)
ISBN: 978-1-4697-9172-2 (ebk)

Printed in the United States of America

iUniverse rev. date: 02/04/2013

CONTENTS

To Korly and Nate
For everything you both give and teach me, every moment.
I was stirred to get back to the shore to be fully present for you which
taught me I had to be fully present for me.

INTRODUCTION

In April of 2009, I decided to pursue Co-Active Life Coaching as a career after borrowing the course text book from a girlfriend and devouring the first two chapters within 48 hours. I empathetically nodded through the chapters, feeling like "Wow—this was meant for me". And then I completed my first text book exercise that blasted me out of the fog I had been living in and proceeded to clearly identify where I was dropping the ball(s) in my life. I jumped in, signed up and completed the coaching courses, as well as the extensive multi-faceted certification program and examinations.

Let me start by providing some perspective to the context in which this book is written. Often when people hear "coaching", they think of coaching in a traditional coaching sense, involving directing or leading someone to an objective or goal. Co-Active Coaching is different from this in a variety of ways. The Coaches Training Institute (CTI) suggests that *Co-Active Coaching is about believing that people are naturally creative, resourceful and whole—completely capable of finding their own answers to whatever challenges they face. The role of a Co-Active Coach® is to ask powerful questions, listen and empower to elicit the skills and creativity a client already possesses, rather than instruct or advise.* (1)

The experience from my Co-Active Coaches Training was different from anything I had either participated in or facilitated for others and allowed me the platform to learn a ton about myself. My learning occurred through a number of different mediums including self-reflection, reading, skill drills, journaling and more. Through Co-Active Coaches Training, my role as facilitator evolved which led participants to approach me after my speaking engagements, encouraging me to capture my thoughts and learnings on paper, so the nuggets from my own experience would be passed to others. This is how I arrived at writing this book. *The Happy Place* captures stories, insights and questions to assist you the reader to find your Happy Place or best position for ultimate life living. For myself, my Happy Place is when I am where I ultimately want to live my life. It's equivalent to the state of mind I have when I am enjoying the shore line; the feel of the sand under my feet, the wind in my hair, the rhythmic sound of the waves colliding, the fresh smell of the ocean and the warmth of the sun on my skin all give me an 'ahhhh' like nothing else has in my life (to the present date that is!). And when I am in my Happy Place I am fully present to my senses, and more importantly acutely aware of what's important to me. The Happy Place is a clear state of mind for me; my values are zinging and my life awareness is deep.

My perspective of *The Happy Place* is about being fully present in my life. The topics included in this book are all things I have explored to keep me in this *Happy Place* connection on a daily basis, regardless of the day. This book has been created to provide you, the reader, your own paced self-exploration. Questions I've asked myself or have been asked as I've delved through the process to find my Happy Place connection have been included for your own exploration. Each chapter ends with questions for you to dive deeper with, if so inclined. Will you take the challenge of finding your equivalent *Happy Place*? The bigger question may be—What will it cost you if you don't?

Enjoy the read. Giggle through my experiences, be aware of my vulnerabilities, feel my trust. Then pony up with yours—I dare you.

Second Edition Note:

I decided to do a second edition to The Happy Place for a couple reasons:

1- *Through feedback and insight from First Edition Readers it was important to me to tweak and adjust with their learnings*

2- *My journey continued. And there were enough of my own 'WOW' moments that I wanted to ensure the book direction properly captured them to assist with your journey.*

3- *New chapters. This links to both point two and the grin on my face now.*

4- *Regardless of how many eyes have reviewed this, typos continued to be found. For this I apologise and thank you for sending in any you come across.*

Warmly & With Gratitude

Nance XO

How to use this book

So . . . my introduction just encouraged you to give this a full chance and you're still reading. This is a good sign!

This book is an "experience book". Yep—that's a home-grown term and its meaning is this: the book is an interactive book, like a workbook, which allows you the reader to actively participate in steering the journey and also reaping the result(s). The chapter topics in this book are introduced in a maximum of eleven pages. At the end of every presented topic you will find questions for you to record your response to, reflect on, or develop. That's where you come in.

I can sit and write *ad nauseam* about my experiences and learning, but what impact will that have on you finding your Happy Place? Yes, reading my perspective might give you some laughs and 'a-ha!' moments, but you need to participate to find your own Happy Place. No one's going to hand it over on a silver platter. However, with the rapture I hold for my journey to date I'm being vulnerable and sharing some of the steps I took to reconnect with my Happy Place, functioning in my daily life from my perspective of 'on the shore', with the potential of helping you reconnect with yours.

The style of questions you will find in this book are coaching questions. They come from a place of curiosity, not judgment. I don't have the answers and I don't know what the findings will be for you. What I do know is that if we don't try, we don't know. And the journey will give us lots to build and grow from.

When coaching, we find value in questions. Some questions work for clients, some don't. But to challenge you: if you choose not to answer a question, ask yourself, "What's here for me that I'm avoiding?" There's value in discomfort. Stay in the awkwardness of the discomfort. See what you uncover. I offer to you the same perspective for the different chapters in the book. Some you will initially feel you get more from than others. Only if you experience it versus skip it, will you know.

Lastly—this book is for you to explore at your own pace. Some questions will be a straight-forward answer for you. Others might knock you on your butt for a week. My one-on-one client coaching sessions are usually 45 minutes because that is a good amount of time of focused energy for a client to connect and 'make progress' with whatever topic they're focused on. I share that insight as a time touchstone for you. There's no finish line, just a journey. The key is to take the journey and absorb the experience for what it is. *The Happy Place* is about you exploring you. Be cognizant to not get stuck on the solve/action/fix/do. Explore what you need to be in touch with.

Grab a writing device, get comfortable and commit to doing this for yourself. It's time. Today.

1

"LET ME INTRODUCE MYSELF"

I was recently facilitating a training session with a group of twenty-five employees all from the same company, and part of a large organization. Knowing we'd be working with each other for the full day I started with introductions to 'break the ice' for our initial connection and help set the tone for the day. The task—everyone was asked to introduce themselves in 30 seconds or less. Thirty seconds, depending on the situation, is not a lot of time. Here's a sample of what people shared:

"Hi my name is _____. I've been working at _____ for six years in the role of _____. I live in _____ and am the parent of two teenage boys, Sam and Pete.

Hello. My name is _____. I'm a National Account Manager and have been in this role for 5 months. I transferred from the Vancouver office and so far so good."

Is this similar to what you would say if you asked to introduce yourself to a group of people? Take 30 seconds and think about what your introduction would be.

What struck me from my session that day was what wasn't said. The examples shared above are roles we play in life, important roles. But what we often skip is who we really are. Think about it . . . who are you really?

I ask you this question as openly as I ask it to myself. And I'm exploring it because I believe that although many times in life we think we have the best intentions, we sometimes (often?) lose focus on our own values and life priorities—the stuff that we love, that energises us, that makes us tick and inspires us to live this life as we, individually, want.

Prior to this chapter I would introduce myself stating something like.

"Hi. I'm Nancy Milton. I'm a coach, facilitator and author. I have two energetic boys and I love outdoor activities."

See! We talk about what we do yet not who we are. We acknowledge the roles we play yet not what makes us . . . us.

Pushing myself to explore more of who I am, here's my starter list:

- I listen without judgement and can be counted on (from commitments to birthday cards) by family and friends alike.
- It scares me how much I love ice cream. It can make my day. I love the texture, its coolness and its ability to make me smile at first taste.
- The outdoors makes me tick. Fresh air is like fresh perspective for me. It clears my head, it de-stresses me, and it reminds me of what's important to me. Jogging in the morning is like lining me up with my life priorities. Walking at night allows me a release of the day in order to have a restful sleep.
- I am a closet car singer. I'm terrible, but I love it, and have vowed to sign up for singing lessons by September 2013. I want to learn to sing one of my favourite songs in key. Who knows . . . maybe it will become my life's theme song!
- I am committed to living my life without regret and am one of the most honest people you will ever meet. I share what I am feeling and lead with my heart often.
- Reading is something to which I treat myself. Nothing better than a good book to immerse myself in. Reading is something I need to continue to do more of. It's like "soul nourishment" for me.
- After a 20-year hiatus I am back on the tennis court. Although I am consciously incompetent, it's been a thrill to start the game again and I'm keen to get better at it!

- Parenting is the hardest thing I've ever done . . . and considering I've bungee jumped, sky dived and ran marathons that says something. I love it & am challenged by it frequently.
- Being vulnerable. I define vulnerability as the courage to lose. If I am open to and living that life value every day, then I am at my best because I am willing to put myself out there to experience it. And I continue to push myself to learn how to experience something without concern of getting it right the first time.
- Try is a word I steer clear from as an 'attempted' action word. 'I will or I won't', 'I'm in or I'm out'.
- And as my sweet friend Julie simply reminded me, "You're Nancy". Period.

That's a start on me. Now—who are you? What are you really about? Describe one of your life's favourite moments and what are you prepared to do to get more of them? What makes you laugh like a kid? What do you dream about? What's your ultimate dream?

Explore, enjoy and give it back to yourself. You deserve it.

QUESTIONS FOR YOU TO PLAY IN:

If you were to introduce yourself in 'typical' fashion, what would you share about yourself to others, in 30 seconds or less?

_____

_____

_____

_____

_____

_____

_____

_____

What makes you tick?

_____

_____

_____

_____

_____

_____

_____

_____

What do you most enjoy in life?

_____

_____

_____

_____

_____

_____

_____

_____

Favourite Pastimes (list them all—regardless of how long ago you last partook!)

_____

_____

_____

_____

_____

_____

_____

_____

Favourite Moment (AND what did it give you)?

_____

_____

_____

_____

_____

_____

_____

_____

What are you REALLY about?

_____

_____

_____

_____

_____

_____

_____

_____

When you are at your best you are _____.
(Complete this sentence on the space below with anything and everything that comes to mind!)

_____

_____

_____

_____

_____

_____

_____

_____

From the exploration you just completed, introduce yourself a second time. Now what would you share in 30 seconds or less? Write down that second introduction and record what makes you YOU.

_____

_____

_____

_____

_____

_____

_____

_____

_____

2

THE WORD *SHOULD*

Should sucks. Really, it totally does. I have been 'shoulding' my whole life. "You should call your grandma (daily), you should make a proper dinner (versus serving myself a great plate of nachos with cheese and salsa), you should clean the garage, you should get up, showered and dressed before the kids interrupt the process, you should be HAPPY—what's wrong with you!" See what I mean? There's a whole "here's how it's supposed to be done" guilt part of life that, to put it bluntly, I'm tired of. So, I'm letting go of 'should', and have reintroduced 'must-tick'. And today, I will make the introduction to you.

I'm a morning person. Pre-kids, I would set the alarm in the morning (it's amazing I still remember this, it seems so long ago). When the alarm would go off (music, no shrilling "GET UP" ringing for me), I'd simply lie there for a couple minutes. Listen to the news from the radio, open my eyes, do the mental check list of the body parts (and ailments), LOVE the feeling of the bed comforter cocooning me and the moments of pleasure without a to-do list running through my head like nails on a chalk board.

I gave this up 8+ plus years ago. This five minutes of bliss. This 'connect with my mind/body/spirit regime' and all its benefits to instead thrust myself out of bed—to the point of sometimes dizziness—to begin the marching orders of my 'should' routine for that day.

Then, one morning it all changed. The kids "slept in" (for clarity, this is anytime after 7:00am) and I woke up independently. I listened to the birds chirping. I stretched. I replayed the dream I woke from in my mind. I enjoyed a couple moments of "ahhh'. Then it hit me. I'VE MISSED THIS. I NEED this back in my life. Then my inner voice started with the 'shoulds'. *"You're now behind schedule. You should get dressed FAST. You should make the bed, put on your make up, wake the kids and you should do it without seeming frantic because you're LATE."*

Let me ask you this, does your inner voice know my inner voice?

This particular morning, I put a stop to it.

Simply. I didn't should.

Instead I now 'Must-Tick'.

So, the kids come in within minutes of this blissful experience and my five-year-old literally asks me "Mommy what are you doing in bed?!?". I laugh out loud at his shock that in fact Mommies sleep too. I then asked them to both climb in bed with me so I can teach them to 'Must-Tick'. So they climb in and I prepared them for the "experience" (worded more kid-friendly than what you're about to read now). *"Would you like to start every morning with a couple minutes giggling in bed? Would it be joyous to gaze out the bedroom window and enjoy the beauty of the start of the day? Would it be a better day to feel a connection (to self or each other) before throwing back the covers to rush to get to school and/or work?"*

It's no shock to you I am sure, that the boys' answers to each 'Must-Tick' question were YES. So now, every morning they climb in my bed to 'wake me up'. Looking through my bedroom window, we come up with figures and shapes within the clouds in the sky out my window, we marvel at the colours in the sunrise, we talk about our dreams, we talk about our day to be, or how the tooth fairy makes her way around the globe in the span of a night. Something I have recently added to this discussion is the "what makes you YOU" game. We each take turns talking about the things we see in ourselves and each other that makes us who we are. We connect. And the alarm is set for a specific time to allow us to wake each other up and have this 'must-tick' time in case anyone ever oversleeps again (ha . . . have only needed that alarm once).

Everyday my life was full of 'shoulds'. I 'should' empty the dishwasher. I 'should' get the laundry to the drycleaners. I 'should' go the neighbour's holiday party. I 'should' make a homemade dessert for Stephanie's pot-luck on Tuesday. What I didn't realise was that most of my life had become "should" rather than "must-ticks". Really, I was 'shoulding' all over myself!!!* And what became really clear to me is that the 'shoulds' lacked emotion. Actually, let me improve the impact of that statement. The 'shoulds' I was completing held nothing but pressure. No feelings, no connection, no want. The impact of this can be huge because 'shoulding' can shut us down, causing us to act and be less than we are capable of. 'Must-Ticks' on the other hand are what keep the skip in our step or the sparkle in our eye. 'Must-Ticks' are things we need to do to keep us connected to who we are.

Now I've got lots of 'shoulds' in my life that I've relabelled with 'must-ticks'. For the rest of them, I do my 'would like to' test to help me better access if the *'should'* is a *'Must-Tick'*. If it's not a 'Must-Tick' I then ask myself, what would be best in the situation? Or what would the benefit be for me to do that in the short- and long-term? What would this do to make my day, or another's day, better/brighter/easier? Then I let my gut answer. My gut (like yours!) is always right, it's the interpretation of my gut I've been screwing up on. What 'shoulds' are 'Must-Ticks' in your life? And what 'shoulds' need to experience the 'would like to' filter to give your life connection back?

Before I let you get started I think it's important to have a starting point. My friend Crista read a draft version of *The Happy Place* & she said *"I find this section confusing—what are "Must-Ticks"—I mean really?? In my mind they are the basics for living (food, shelter, clothing . . . ok, and sex . . .)—is there an opportunity to get people to dig deeper to define what a "Must-Tick" really is?"* I like Crista's question and I agree with her 'Must-Tick' list. Her list is your starting point and lightly speaks to the 'Maslow Hierarchy of Needs' list. (2) The difference between Maslow's list, Crista's, mine, and yours is that you need to OWN yours. Be specific. Know your 'Must-Ticks'. For example looking at our need for food; specifically is it that you need to eat & will eat anything for any meal, that you need three balanced, homemade meals a day or something different? Are you settling on takeout food for two meals a day & paying for it in calories, energy and dollars yet, accepting it? What category does food nutrition fall in for you—should, Must-Ticks or would like to? It's time to get clear on what your 'Must-Ticks', what are your 'shoulds' and what are your 'would like to's' for each of your basic needs? Be clear on them. It's time to live by them.

Please note: Since writing the first edition of The Happy Place I have learned from readers that author & speaker Tony Robbins and Loretta LaRoche also use this term "shoulding on ourselves". And my guess is there are more of us out there! I was in a coaching session when it "came" to me. Please use it as your own screen tool as I am sure Tony & Loretta would encourage you to as well.

QUESTIONS FOR YOU TO PLAY IN:

What 'shoulds' are 'Must-Ticks' in your life? And what adjustments will you make, to make them easier to complete/ be more efficient/ include fun?

_____
_____
_____
_____
_____
_____
_____
_____

What do you need to have more of in your day? (If stuck refer to you list of "enjoys" from the first chapter in this booked called "Let me introduce myself")

My Must-Ticks include:

_____
_____
_____
_____
_____
_____
_____

What are you now aware of wanting for yourself? Outline below what that looks like.

_____

_____

_____

_____

_____

_____

_____

_____

Having any four things you listed above, what improvement will you feel in your daily being?

_____

_____

_____

_____

_____

_____

Which two Must-Tick items will you begin to have (or put a plan in place to have) today?

1. _____

2. _____

And making sure you have space for these wonderful Must-Ticks, which 4 shoulds will you stop, immediately?

1. _____

2. _____

3. _____

4. _____

3

Finding your 'You' list

I'm just going to put it out there—I'm divorced. Yep. There are a gazillion sub-topics that I could write about from this experience. Today's topic: How do we give everyone else what I've experienced from getting divorced? An allocated amount of "you time". *Please note—I'm fully aware that every divorce is different and there are many variables involved. I am speaking specifically from my own experience and speaking to the amount of time my children are allocated to be with their father leaving me with a chunk of 'childless' time in my month.* Let me take a step back.

In the parenting agreement the we developed, my children's father has our kiddies every-other-weekend. On the weekends that I don't have the children, you name it, I'm making it happen: dinner with girlfriends, walks or lunches with other friends, learning how to sand and stain my hardwood floors (and then deciding to pay someone else to do it), trying new recipes, signing up for new activities and reconnecting with some favourites that needed dusting off! This past Saturday morning I did a 70-minute elliptical 'ride' followed by a 90 minute tennis cardio clinic. I HAVEN'T PLAYED TENNIS FOR 20 YEARS . . . and it is literally thrilling for me to be out there again. And that was before 11 o'clock! When friends ask me what I've got on for a weekend that I am without the kids . . . I've learned to stop listing my 'time for me' plan a third of the way through because of the jaw-dropping envy they have. So my question is—how do we give everyone else this 'mandatory chunk of time for self'?

I write about this 'time for me' plan because like any North American who has functioned for a week with a group of people with multiple role deliverables (a.k.a. spouse, employee, parent, soccer coach, charity volunteer canvasser, etc), I'm pretty aware of the stress levels that many people live with on this continent. Look around you—how many of your friends are actually 'looking for things to do' because they have spare time?! I was at a work lunch last week and one of the guests was referring to a show she watches when she's bored. "Bored?" I think this is the first adult I've ever met who, other than talking about a poorly-run meeting, has used this word.

I'm fortunate enough to have this "free time" pass handed to me and say "Heck—you've got 48 hours for yourself, what do you choose?". Yes—I have chores to do, work to complete, errands to run and quite frankly two gorgeous boys to miss that squeezes at my heart . . . but, I owe it to myself to refuel myself. And I owe it to my sons to be as connected to my core being as possible when they get back home to me. So I chunk out my 48 hours of time for optimal usage, including two good night sleeps, so that we can reap the benefits of being separated when we're back together again. You most likely won't have 48 hours for 'time for me' every second week. What I'm challenging you to look at is in fact, do you give yourself any? The only person who can give this to you is you. It's your responsibility to stay connected with yourself. And by being connected with yourself, you will impact your other relationships, because you will be more content.

So I ask you, what can you do today (regardless of your life status) to give yourself some REAL time for you? Errands don't count. Neither does laundry. Both are things off your to-do list which usually only give us temporary celebration or joy. Both those items can go on your 'shoulds' list from the last chapter. I mean something good! What "makes you tingle" to have it back in your life again? And how much time will it really take out of your week? Two hours? Four? Aren't you worth it? You know how I know I am worth it? Because I haven't stopped talking about tennis since I left the court Saturday. I FLIPPIN' LOVE BEING OUT THERE ON THE COURT! And let me manage your expectations—I am VERY consciously incompetent when it comes to my tennis skill! This has nothing to do with me winning matches or being good at the game. Not at all. Instead—this experience is about doing something truly for me, and by doing that, what it gives to all other aspects of my life. Every other weekend I have 48 hours. How much time will you give yourself?

And starting today, what are you going agree to do for you? The only person who will do it for you is you.

Last comment. I drafted this chapter 3 years ago. It was one of the first chapters I captured and I wrote it because of the impact putting me back into my life and onto my priority list was making. It was sparking something in me that I hadn't felt for awhile, too long in fact. So, three years later I'm at a different level again. I have learned how to bring me as a priority into my life AND how to bring that together with the life around me. Once I learned how to 'fill my tank' on my own time, I began to practise the skill while I am with others (for example with my boys). As I shared with you in the first chapter I love the outdoors. Bringing my enjoyment of the outdoors, family time and Canadian snow together, I'm renting a chalet for the winter. The boys and I are having a hoot on the ski hill, quality family chat and play time and I am filling my tank. All at the same time! The chalet environment is giving us the space to hang out and be together different than our space at home. Each weekend north is like a mini vacation for us, me included. It's truly wonderful. In reflection I realise I had to both learn and practise the skill of giving to myself before I could include others. Some would call that baby steps. I call it progress. YAH! Neat is that I have a number examples I could now share with you on this. The habit has been started. Now, let's get yours started.

QUESTIONS FOR YOU TO PLAY IN:

If I, the new magic fairy in your life, could give you a free week of "anything you want" what would it be? Don't be shy—make a mega list of wants. "GO BIG BABY!"

_____

_____

_____

_____

_____

_____

_____

_____

_____

_____

_____

_____

_____

_____

Ok—now go back up to the list and circle your top five. And if you didn't come up with at minimum 10 ideas here, go back to the first chapter in this book called 'Let me introduce myself' (approximately page 4). Read what you recorded there. When you've got some gems, come back to this page.

Next, list the five 'wants' you circled as priorities, in the left column. In the other two columns record a) what having this would give you and b) what you need to make it happen

	5 things I'd like to have (more of) in my life	What would you gain by doing this?	What will you do make this happen?
1			
2			
3			
4			
5			

Go to http://lifedots.ca/connect-with-your-dots-template/ for larger printable worksheets.

Lastly, looking at the list you created, which two will you put an action plan to TODAY to start giving this to yourself?

Chosen priority	Plan to make it happen (elaborate from what you wrote above so what you specifically need to do is clear)	Timing and Commitment
1		
2		

CONGRATULATIONS

You now have started to reconnect with yourself more than you were yesterday. It's only the beginning, and we're only on chapter 3! Go get your calendar and add these timelines and commitments to your calendar. And a suggestion for those of you concerned about not sticking to it. Choose someone in your life that you will report into on these commitments, support you and also hold you to the consequence if you don't stick to your commitment. Who can assist you with accountability on this? Whoever it is, call them now. No time like the present . . .

Heck, maybe your ask will get them thinking about what they can be doing for themselves.

EXTENDED WASHROOM BREAK

Laugh all you like but when I first started facilitating, before I would get in front of the room to facilitate a session, instead of doing what I now consider is my job (mingling with the participants at their seats, introducing myself, etc) I delayed the participant connection and would take an extended washroom break. Yep. I would slowly head to the washroom, even though I've already been twice prior to setting up my session room and putter around in there until show time (show time for the start of my training session that is!)

Guess who would lose when I took the extended washroom break?

Everyone.

My participants lost because I didn't carry through on my responsibilities as the session leader.

I lost because I discarded the opportunity to start my session off at a 10; to be fully present with my audience (KEY when it comes to communication) and I didn't start building trust with them from the first available opportunity. Know what was stopping me? Nerves/ Fear. You know what I'm talking about. We all have it. And you might have it right now reading this.

There is the potential for a reader of this book to float through the starting chapters like an extended washroom break.

It's commitment time. Are you fully present to the experience this book brings?

Somehow you got this book. Maybe you bought it, someone gave it to you or you saw me at a speaking engagement once and were given one for being in the room. What interests me is that you've read 15 pages already. I personally stop by page four if I can't get into a book . . . . yet here you are.

Since I can't see your book, nor am I the 'micro author' hanging over your shoulder ensuring you are filling every blank line with crafty responses, I have a question for you.

Have you decided to:

a) Thoroughly and honestly answer the questions I asked you in chapters one through three?
b) Wimp out on living your own life to its fullest and are using this book like a Yellow Pages directory? (Taking only what you need at the time and then shoving it back on the counter until you're in 'must have' mode again).
c) Answer the 'easy' questions only?
d) Other: _____
e) Apply all of the above, depending on my mood during time of reading.

What do you lose by not fully answering the questions?

Another perspective—What are you willing to gain by answering the questions?

It's time. Join me. Join the ride.

4

What's your Ride like?

So the book introduction spoke to one of my 'reality check' moments that came through an introspective exercise in my coaching manual. I share this tool with you, with permission from CTI, The Coaches Training Institute (3). It is called "The Wheel of Life" (see page 21 for visual of exercise) and my explanation of the exercise to a coaching client goes something like this:

To help better understand you and get you to where you want to go, it's helpful to know where you currently are in your major life components. It's sort of like taking a life inventory. Think of it this way—if you got to the grocery store without knowing what you have in your fridge, you might overstock on items that can go bad, or you may miss buying an essential and end up having to make a second trip to pick up this staple or go without. And speaking for myself only, there are some staples I'm not prepared to go without!

The Wheel of Life exercise depicts major life areas for a typical person—things that people would describe as important to them, or key areas of focus.

These areas include:

Health
Family and Friends
Fun and Recreation
Personal Growth
Physical Environment
Money

Significant Other and Romance
Career

The Wheel of Life key components or *spokes* can be modified to reflect different areas if needed, yet, in my experience I have found that we've been able to capture various 'add-ons' within already set spokes. For example, community connection is important to me so I capture that under Physical Environment. A coaching client wanted to capture her role as Mother separately and so decided to split the Career spoke down the middle 50% for her role of Mother and 50% for continuing to stay networked and immersed in her industry while she was at home full time with her children.

Let me provide you some insight on each of the eight areas before you complete the exercise:

Personal Growth—What are you doing to continue to develop yourself? After an insane ride with "baby brain" post delivery of my children, to get myself back to my *career* standard of mind, I took on the project of reading a non-fictional book every month. This is something that's helped to keep me at a certain professional level within my industry and be able to continue to bring latest trends and knowledge to my sessions. Also—it keeps me fresh and connected to my want of 'always be learning'. Other examples of personal growth include skill courses, getting/ having a mentor, working with a coach and job shadowing.

Physical Environment—This area refers to your home environment. Does your home badly need a renovation—to the point you're disconnected with your living space? Are you getting what you need from your neighbourhood? Does your home give you what you need to be happy there? Our home can reflect back to us who we are and this is also where we come to 'be' (share meals, sleep, be with family and friends, relax, enjoy intimacy etc). Some kids have a favourite stuffed animal or blanket they sleep with. A guy I dated in high school had a favourite t-shirt that although beyond wear-able outside, he lived in this 'holey shirt' in his house. This type of comfort is similar to what you can obtain from your Physical Environment. Home can be many things . . . a few are: safe, comforting, relaxed, warm, soothing, energy, clean, yours. First you need to be aware of what you need from your home. Then consider whether or not you have what you need from your Physical Environment and understand how that is impacting you. Also physical environment can be a place where you spend a lot of time and your connection to it. School may be an example of this, a car for those who drive a lot for their jobs (i.e. sales reps, drivers/ delivery roles) and work for those who are actually at their office more than their home.

Money—This isn't "do you have enough?" but instead think of it as overall financial. What's your budget like? What's money stress like for you? Are you in debt? Do you have liabilities, bills, credit? What about income? Savings? Investments & Assets? How are your financial management skills, your shopping and spending? Do you think about abundance or lack of money?

Fun and Recreation—Are you getting enough play time in your life? Hiking, tennis, skiing, giggling, travel . . . you know your list . . . how much of this list are you actually getting to enjoy in a week? What about hobbies, nature, relaxing, socializing, joy in your life? What's your fun-thermometer at these days? If you are unclear on what your fun list is, go back to Chapter One and read what you answered for "what makes you tick?" question found on page 3.

Family and Friends—Are you getting to connect with them consistently enough for your needs? Do you have enough friends and family or do you need more? Do you have too many to keep up with and are therefore 'losing' time for another life area like fun and recreation? Do you have any you need to let go of? What friends are you holding on to because you share history together yet no longer have anything in common with?

Career—What is your dream 'if I could do ANYTHING' career? Are you content in the job/role you currently hold? Is it in-line with the career map or plan you've created to end up where you'd like to be? Do you like what you do? Or is your current job where you want to be? Is it even a stepping stone on the path to where you want to end up?

Significant Other and Romance—Is your relationship working for you? Are your needs being met? Do you want to be in a relationship, currently aren't and are exhausted from looking? Or presently you're not in a relationship and are satisfied without one?

Health—How would you summarise your health? Are you eating properly? Working out a minimum of three times a week? Sleeping 7-8 hours a night? What's your stress level like?

On the next page you will find the Wheel of Life exercise. First read, then follow the instructions provided. Take one minute to complete the exercise. There is no right answer. No one is judging your response. Be honest. Be truthful. Answer from your gut.

*Please note the Wheel of Live exercise is used by Coaches with permission from The Coaches Training Institute. The Wheel of Life exercise is referred to throughout this book, in reference to your experience with the template within this Chapter.

WHEEL OF LIFE EXERCISE

The 8 sections in the Wheel of Life represent Balance. Seeing the center of the wheel as 0 and the outer edge as 10, rank your level of satisfaction with each life area by drawing a straight or curved line to create a new outer edge (see sample). The new perimeter of the circle represents YOUR Wheel of Life.

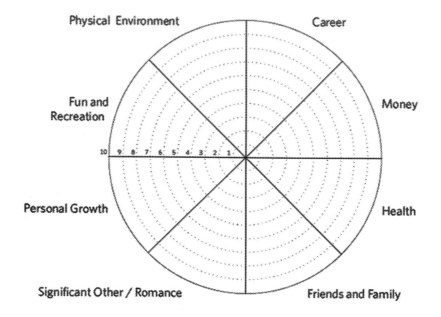

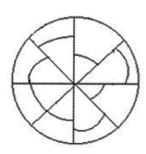

Example of what your wheel may look like

Go to http://lifedots.ca/connect-with-your-dots-template/ for larger printable worksheets.

WHAT'S YOUR RIDE LIKE? *(CONTINUED)*

Once you've joined the lines from the eight areas to form your personal wheel, reflect: if you were to take a long ride on this wheel, what would your ride be like? (i.e. smooth, bumpy, stalled, unable to move forward with any consistency, etc)

Record your reflection here. Additional questions to help you ponder: What surprises you looking at your life this way? What's your initial reaction to your wheel?

_____

_____

_____

_____

_____

_____

_____

_____

_____

_____

_____

_____

_____

_____

_____

_____

This exercise is a tool to illustrate how satisfied one is in their life. A client I was working with completed marking her satisfaction responses she looked at me bewildered and said "now what?!" Like in coaching, the client is the one with the answers, not (me) the coach. Therefore, what you do with your answers and how you interpret your answers, is up to you. As a coach I use this as a barometer with my clients when we start and finish our coaching relationship. It provides a good touchstone for where the client is with their life and assists with coaching topics if the client gets stuck.

I share the tool with you as your own touchstone for satisfaction in your life. Time mark your Wheel of Life exercise for the day you completed it. To assist you with thinking through the process of what your result means to you, I'll give you some insights of what/how others saw their results.

- Sometimes clients assume that everything should be a ten. Anything below that is not okay and they have changes to make. One may suggests those are high expectations for you. My take is that I think it's important to set standards for yourself so . . . what is realistic? What will push you just out of your comfort zone yet bring you happiness? Is that 7.5 in every wheel spoke? 9 perhaps? And what would the number you want look like, in every wheel spoke (i.e. 8 in all areas)? I am a big believer in visualization. If you can't picture what you want, how can you perform and reach to that? Spend some time thinking about both what you want and what it looks like.

- Some clients assume that whichever area they gave the lowest satisfaction rating to is the first area of focus for coaching. The lowest-rated area might not be the beacon to start with. It might be an indicator of a number of things, but another area might require more urgent attention first. Or it might be low because of what's going on in another area. i.e. *Money* might be rated lowest yet, *Career* is the chosen focus by the client because they have been out of work for two years and are working a minimum wage job to bring in some money. You have an opportunity to reflect on your answers and also look at how they impact the other sections of your wheel.

- Clients may use the Wheel exercise as an inventory of their life. I've seen shock before like "wow . . . I knew I wasn't happy but this is eye opening" or "hmmm . . . I'm in a better spot than I realised."

- Me, I'm looking to have a balanced level of satisfaction in all areas so I aim for a range that varies by 1.5. and have created targets within each to assist me to maintaining the life I want to have (for the most part!) daily. Also, I have learned by my own Wheel of Life experience just how important your values being linked to your wheel sections are. If there is a disconnect with your values & your wheel spokes, you might as well pull over because regardless of your efforts, your wheel won't get the traction you need to move in any direction.

Remember—there is no right or wrong response to the Wheel of Life. It's the Wheel of YOUR life. Listen to your gut. Really listen. Mmmhhhmm . . . that's what the wheel is doing for you; holding the mirror so you can see all sides. What will you do to action what you want OR stay where you are because it's GOOD. There's a great book my boys have. It's called 'Don't let the Pigeon Drive the Bus" by Mo Willems (4). Looking at the wheel being a steering wheel of a car versus a mode of transportation—who is driving your bus? Who's navigating? Who's holding the map? And is there someone yelling directions at you from the 'cheap' seats in the back? Remind me—if it's your bus, who MUST be the Driver? Only you know where you want to go.

As you continue through this book, different life areas will be your focus. Challenge yourself to be with whatever is there for you to sift through. Balance your ride.

5

REAL

An acknowledgement I've been consistently hearing from people over the last three years is that "I'm real". It's interesting, the impact it's had on me. Love goes through me when I hear this. I extract from the acknowledgement that I've been fully present in the conversation that I am sharing with the other person, that they can both tell and feel that I am standing 'fully rooted' in who I am with inner strength and lastly—that my vulnerabilities are apparent and I'm smiling about it! I'm being true to myself and what I believe is important. I also think there is a link between being real and being authentic which others may call being themselves. (Background on me—I use to be a Master Multi-Tasker—details on MMT in chapter 20). I have worked diligently at being fully present in more life moments versus completing the task(s) within the moments and missing the moments completely. My one-liner on this is that I'm now about "more being and less doing" in my life.

This acknowledgement from others also brings me to wonder both "what is real?" and "what would allow people to be real with both themselves and others?" My definition of this interpretation of real is that who I am is clear when you are speaking with me. I wonder if for people to acknowledge that I am real suggests that this is something that people might not see fully in many other people, to the point it stands out enough that they are acknowledging it in me. So IF that is the case, what is everyone holding back on? And what's keeping this held back?

In my life experiences, when I have held back on me (either not being true to myself, my values or my needs/taking care of myself) I have lost. Either the experience hasn't been what it could have been and it ends up being one of those I reflect on in following days/months/years or I think "oh . . .

wow, here's what could have been a completely different outcome". On the other hand, in the past when I went with my gut, my heart and my clear head—TA DA!—real. AND the experience was a valuable one.

So what makes us hold back? Act certain ways? Respond certain ways? Are we concerned about saying the right thing? Is it easier to speak at surface topic levels versus what we're truly thinking/feeling/knowing? And—in case you're looking to me to give you these answers . . . I can't. And not because I'm holding back on you, but instead because I think we all have different responses to these questions specific to the situation and to us as individuals. My answers for what can push or pull me from my 'real zone' are different than yours and the next reader.

What I will share with you is my life vow:

I'm sticking with real.

Because since I made my fully present life vow, my life has improved ten-fold.

I am happier, I feel connected to my being and to what's important to me.

I am more relaxed yet more focused on my priorities.
I am parenting my children better and I am laughing more. I laughed before, yet now, my laugh comes from the gut. It feels great.
I attract more people. Good people. People I'm keen to share both time and connection with.

My perspective on being real is about connecting with my gut. I listen to it now versus interpreting wrongly and tripping over myself. A girlfriend of mine Sue shared a learning with me from a book she had read called "The Gift of Fear" by Gavin Becker (5). She shared that the author explained that humans are the only species taught *not* to go by their instincts. How flippin' foolish does that sound?! Yet, I agree. We often don't lead with our gut and are taught instead to do things 'this way'. Think about how this applies to you. It starts young for most of us. You're 5 years old and being hosted for dinner at a friend of your parents. Your parent whispers under their breathe that, "It doesn't matter that you don't want any more to eat.

You are not to be rude but instead to eat every morsel of the plate you were served by our host." Yes. We learned the anti-gut rule at an early age. Yeesh . . . That rule has not served me well in my life. How has it served you?

To get started on this "REAL business", let's look at some basic examples covering compliments, greetings and apologies. We'll start with the compliment versus the acknowledgment. First, I think there is a place in conversations for both.

I use to compliment people frequently. If I saw something that caught my eye, I complimented the beholder on it i.e. "I like your sweater." "Your eyes are a beautiful shade of green." "Love your shoes—where did you get them?" This is a way in which some people approach reaching others, me (back then) included. Interesting learning for me—I thought this was a special way I got in touch with others. Participating in some coach training I realised that I personally lacked between defining an acknowledgement and a compliment. My easy tip to help filter the difference is that a compliment often speaks to the outside of you like the examples I listed above. Literally something that can be seen through a visual (what you look like; clothing, eyes, hair, etc) and not an action. Acknowledgements often speak to what comes from the inside. For example, "Your honesty is commendable", "I acknowledge your determination to making this situation better", and "You are a person of integrity and kindness that reaches everyone around you."

Read and feel the difference between the examples?

Acknowledgement connects differently. Acknowledgment often reaches a higher landing platform for the person receiving it. It's like "Wow, you've really noticed me. Thank you." My observations suggest that people don't use acknowledgement often. It can tread to areas that lots of people don't easily talk about or get into. Some would see it as the "touchy feely" stuff. I see it as the real stuff. I'm acknowledging your real stuff. Because I like the real stuff. My recap so far—me being real within myself has opened up my awareness of 'real' in others, which is what I acknowledge in people when it touches me.

Will you try this out for 24 hours—to acknowledge as many friends and co-workers you are in contact with. If you struggle with how to phrase it look at it this way "who is he/she being?" and then acknowledge what you witness. Another tip, start with "I acknowledge your _____." to build the skill for yourself. Observe people's response to your new approach. Take in the impact of your statement. My hunch is not only will you impact them; you'll impact you and a value of yours as well. Betcha it will feel closer to REAL than the complement.

Next, let's move to the salutation of others. Often people cordially greet each other with a standard "Hello. How are you?" We were taught at a young age that this is what you said when you initially saw someone or were re-introduced to someone. My question for you—how often do you listen to the response of the person you asked? And to flip it another way—when you are asked, how often do you answer with a real answer? I'm not suggesting you share with an intimate secret with a stranger on the question "how are you?" but, instead I challenge you to play in what you could share, and what difference it might make on both the interaction and your day. Specifically—I ask those I care about how they are because I genuinely am interested in the answer. However the question often is not formed like the traditional "how are you?" If it's a client I'm developing a session for or a potential client the question instead may be "what brings you to our meeting today?" or "What's been going in the last week/month that will influence our time together?" With a friend it may be "I've missed you! Share your Wow-like update with me!" These approaches may seem odd to you. Why, because they are me, not you. Here's my push for you: is 'how are you' *you* or something you *just do*. Make it yours.

My approach (to both what I ask in a greeting and how I respond when I am asked how I am) has impacted me. It has brought my company new business, opened up dating opportunities, introduced me to a number of new friends, and improved retail customer service and restaurant table service, to name a few.

Now—for those I don't know well, may never spend time with again or am sharing a transaction with, I don't ask how they are. In my opinion that conversation isn't going to go far YET I'd be keen to have fun in the interaction so I ask questions that may pertain to the interaction, their job, or simply what's caught my attention in the moment. What's amazing to me is the appreciation from the other person to be spoken with instead of spoken to, the welcome break in their routine day, and the impact of someone else's (mine) genuine interest in them. I recently met a potential new client is a coffee shop to share an information session. After receiving my order the cashier/ server (Aaron) thanked me for 'being polite and nice". He THANKED me. I responded, grinning, explaining that I only treated him the way I guessed HE would want to be treated. Again and again I receive beautiful responses for being real. Lucky me because this is the world I want to live in.

Carry this salutation approach to the use of someone's name. When my boys were 3 and 4 years of age, I taught them to introduce themselves to anyone providing us a service and to ask their name. We practise this skill in our local convenience store, at restaurants with wait staff, the community center, and the library. The dialogue goes something like this:

Korly: "Hi my name is Korly. What's your name?"
Clerk: *slightly thrown off by this gesture* "ummm, Wayne"
Korly: "Hi Mr. Wayne. May I please have a Canadian Maple Doughnut?"

And when Mr. Wayne gives Korly the change from his purchase and the treat:

Korly: "Thank you Mr. Wayne. I wish you a fun day."

I have taught my children to use people's names when we talk to them. Why? My answer; because they are people. It's amazing how much smoother a conversation can go when a name connection has been made. It can take a sterile conversation to a personal one. It can make it real. Interesting to observe the response of the stranger to my children—*insert proud parenting moment sigh here.*

Last, let's tackle the apology. We Canadians are known for our polite Canadian "I'm sorry". I have been caught in the past apologising for things I shouldn't be or really don't need to apologise for. For example, if someone is rushing by me and I don't get out of the way fast enough, I turn and say "Sorry about that". REALLY?!—Shouldn't the bruiser be apologizing for whipping by without a warning? Instead I'm there with my trained response, picking myself off the sidewalk after the collision. Yeesh!

Another interesting use of 'I'm sorry' comes from child's play. Often times as a parent we push hard to have our children apologise for the 'taking your toy, not sharing, smacking you' scenarios yet by the time they achieve the 'spit it out' sorry response there's little meaning to it. Usually at this point the parent of the child 'holding out' on the sorry has apologised profusely to the parent and the 'victim' child . . . . back to the "I'm sorry overkill" experience. Also, referring to the playground scenario, when your kid hits another kid in the playground we teach them to say "I'm sorry." And more children are being taught to <u>not</u> say "it's ok" (because it's not ok you hit me) but instead to say "thank you for apologizing". I like this spin. To me it acknowledges the wrong without taking the apology away from the person or situation hurt.

Then, there's the 'insert the pain someone is going through here' "I'm sorry". Divorce, death of a family member or friend, health issue, etc., we all know the list It's our most common reaction to a tragic/hardship situation when we hear about it. And I get it, we hear about something tough someone else is experiencing and often times are automatic response is "I'm sorry." What I'm sensitive to is whether I'm throwing the "I'm sorry blanket" onto the situation versus spending the time I need to on the situation and/or people involved. Again, many variables impact this response and sometimes I'm sorry is both exactly and all that needs to be said. Yet, sometimes I think it was a 'thrown blanket/ covering' for me and I'm not okay with that anymore. To share an example of my new approach, in a shuttle from the airport recently the driver was sharing with me that his family lives in another country and that he hasn't seen them for 2.5 years because of governing restrictions from his native land. His youngest child is 4 years old. The driver then shared with me that he calls home a couple times a day. His story stopped me in my tracks. Here we were sharing pleasantries (it was a 40 minute drive) and one of my innocent interest questions brought this stranger and I to this spot of pain and heartache for him. Instead of saying I'm sorry, I spoke what I was feeling after literally sitting there tongue tied for at least a minute. It went something like this, "Honestly—I am sitting here with you feeling numb.

I am struggling to find words to acknowledge how hard this must be for you every day. How tough this must be for you and your family both."

The shuttle driver example is from my REAL arena I now play in. I have adjusted my personal use of I'm sorry. Don't get me wrong—"I'm sorry" when used from a head and heart connection is rich. What I'm reflecting includes a couple things:

- When I am sorry, is there a better choice of words that I can use to more fully acknowledge what the person said and therefore acknowledge their feelings and thoughts. For example: "I can hear your frustration. This must be a really trying time for you".
- Is the subject something I should instead be acknowledging versus apologising for?
- What do the words I'm sorry mean to me (when I say them to others)?
- What's the intent when you say "I'm sorry" and what's the impact on the receiver?
- What's my gut say?

Specific to the "I'm sorry" example, **things to ponder:**

- Monitor yourself. How often do you use I'm sorry? A little, a lot, like a band-aid or like the traditional use of good china (rarely).
- Do your words 'I'm sorry' mean anything to the receiver?
- What message do you truly want to convey when you say "I'm sorry"? What do you want the receiver to know from your statement?
- What will you continue to do when it comes to 'I'm sorry'?
- What will you now do differently when it comes to apologising?
- How will you own these adjustments to your current habits, starting now?
- What would you want to know if you were the receiver or in that situation?
- Thinking about your answer to the last question—what would you and the receiver gain by you stating it out loud?

The approach to some of these communication basics—listening to your gut or hunch, greetings, acknowledgements and apologies—and your awareness of your use may help you to move into some new, REAL being fully you and/or fully present territory. A great starting place, and we haven't even touched vulnerabilities yet!

Feel like you've got the communication basics already and want to take real 'deeper'? Firstly—WOW. Sit in feel that for a minute. Acknowledge your own authenticity.

Now, exploring how to go deeper. There are many roads to get to this deeper spot.

A suggested question to the deeper REAL spot is, what's currently easy for you to be REAL at/in/with? What gives you that freedom? What does it feel like? What does it give you when you are this way? And to go deeper with it, how would being like this in other areas of your life give you more of the connected experience you're wanting?

Catch yourself. In various situations daily, ask yourself (using your inner voice) 'Am I being fully present in this moment?' And if the answer is no, stay there and consider what's causing you not to be and what adjustments can be made to change it.

And if you're looking for "more real" in your life here are some **things to ponder:**

- What will I risk losing in my life by not being fully present in my actions and conversations?
- What excuse is it time to free myself from?
- What is sucking the life out of me? What can I add/bring/do in my life to make my heart sing (louder)?
- What impact does pretending to be something I'm not have on my life?

I recently heard a great quote that went something like: Life is like a rollercoaster. You can either scream every time you hit a bump or you can throw your hands in the air and enjoy it. My vote—ENJOY THE RIDE! Put yourself out there, as you, the real you.

QUESTIONS FOR YOU TO PLAY IN

How are you cheating yourself by not giving yourself more REAL moments?

_____

_____

_____

_____

_____

_____

_____

_____

What would you gain if you listened to your heart and gut more and your head less?

_____

_____

_____

_____

_____

_____

_____

_____

What's the worst thing that could happen if you fail?

_____

_____

_____

_____

_____

_____

_____

_____

And what's the best thing that will happen to you if you try and you flop?

_____

_____

_____

_____

_____

_____

_____

_____

6

GIPP

When was the last time you felt truly listened to? This can be indicated when the listener provides the eye contact, the 'lean in' demonstration of interest and the occasional head nod, but I mean more than that. I mean when you can *FEEL* the 'listening to', that what you're saying is being taken in, that you're connecting with the other person on a deeper than 'typical conversation' level, that what you're saying is important to the other person because of their intent to understand what you are saying. When I facilitate Active Listen exercises in my Intentional Communication courses I call this *Level Two Listening*. *Level Two Listening* is when the listener is listening with their thoughts aside and is focused on your agenda, not theirs. They are listening with curiosity, not judgement. They are listening to both the facts and feelings within what you are sharing through your words, tone and body language. Imagine being listened to without any interpretations being made. Daily, I work to apply this skill. Let me explain:

Often times when we are speaking to others we sort what they are saying (their actual statements) with our personal listening filters. (6) Filters are commonly made up of things like generalizations (i.e. all dogs run fasts), interpretations (i.e. Here's my take on what you just said), our personal interests (i.e. If that idea was tweaked just slightly, then it would benefit me as well) and preconceived notions and expectations (i.e. I am sure the last time this happen, things did not turn out the way I wanted them to). I call this screening process GIPP. This happens for a full list of reasons and can easily be steered by things including tone, non-verbal cues like body language, mood, jargon used, and both our past- and current-day personal experiences. And our individual filters can have either a positive or negative impact on how we sieve the information, based on any of the above variables. (7) Geoff Farnsworth of the Relationship Centre suggests to "avoid these filters and (instead) listen with your eyes and ears and heart—just allow others to talk about their experience and responding in a way that shows you got it—changes the whole exchange. We all want to be heard and validated." (8) I agree with Geoff and in this chapter through my examples hope to provide you an increased awareness of your personal filters (GIPP).

Filtering is done (by habit) so often that we often aren't aware of it. Let me share some examples with you:

- A friend of mine wasn't able to breastfeed her newborn baby. After two weeks of health issues, pain and starvation, the mother was told by her Doctor she must move to bottle feeding because her baby just wasn't getting enough nourishment. Even though it was Doctor ordered, my friend still felt tremendous guilt for not being able to breastfeed. In the weeks and months to follow she received the following comments from friends and strangers. "How selfish of you to not nourish your baby with breast milk for its first year of life". "I think breastfeeding is gross. It's nice to see someone not breastfeeding for a change". "How come you're not breastfeeding? Isn't that what you're supposed to do these days?" And yes, all the feedback was unsolicited, received while she was feeding her baby by bottle in public locations and she was going on little to no sleep and just a slight hormonal switch-a-roo in her body! Imagine the impact of the GIPP on her.
- I was fortunate enough to go to Australia, New Zealand and Fiji 12 years ago for eight weeks. For fun, I came home with a fake nose ring and fake belly tattoo (neither nose rings or tattoos were as common place as they are today). My family greeted me with a 10 foot 'Welcome Home Nancy' banner at the airport on the Friday night. The nose ring was not acknowledged until Sunday after dinner when my mother said, "so, when are we discussing your new accessory". The experiment was interesting enough with my family that I decided to try it with the office on Monday. I was working on the agency side of things at a modern-hip organization didn't consider concern about job loss. I had some colleagues approach with lots of questions. "Was it tough to blow

my nose?" "I'm thinking about getting one, did it hurt?". I had others completely ignore it, to the point that when they were speaking to me, they would speak *around* my nose! Then, I had one office employee approach me and state "Nancy, I thought you were an attractive girl. I no longer respect you and I think you have defaced yourself." IMAGINE! On the other end, what 'GIPP' did I have on nose rings? What made this an experiment for me? And when I met my new boss on my first day back (this was a surprise, I didn't know this prior to my arrival Monday morning at the office) I quickly explained the moment we were in a closed door office that the nose ring was fake. Hmmm . . . What was my judgement on people with nose rings? What assumptions of mine did I guess my new boss may impose on me?

Now let's transfer this to the way you listen. Think about it. When you are speaking with someone consider how often you:

- Cut them off with a solution to their problem
- Interrupt them with a similar story of a time when it happened to you
- Make guesses at the outcome of the story while they are telling the story
- Respond with 'why did you do it that way?'
- Half listen, while responding to a BB/email message or going through your personal mental to-do list?

My guess is that you've answered often to at least one of the responses above. We all do it. Yet it sucks for the person who is speaking to us.

Now think about the reverse. Who do you feel in your life Level Two Listens to you? Really listens to what you have to say. Four people spring to my mind straight away when I ponder this. When any of the four people are listening to me, I literally can feel them connecting with me. I feel that what I am saying is important because their attention is fully mine. I share more with them because of their ability to listen. I trust them all immensely and would do anything for any of them because I feel such a bond with them. What does Level Two Listening feel like to you and who's doing it for you? Your turn—when was the last time you fully

Level Two Listened to someone and what's stopping you from being fully present in your conversations?

Listening without interpretation or judgement is an amazing skill. I completely admit that I miss multi-tasking while I'm talking but my relationships are worth it. People notice the difference and I feel more connected to what's important to those people as well as reconnected to my life-value of living more moments fully.

What 'bad' listening habit are you willing to drop? What are you willing to give back in your relationships? Start today—and enjoy the thrill of connection.

SOMETHING TO PLAY IN:

Make today an 'observation of listening' day.

1) When someone is speaking to you, notice what you are listening to—your agenda (stuff in your head) or are you whole-heartedly listening to them?

If you're listening to your head, what's coming up for you? And what are you willing to change to be more present for conversations you're sharing?

2) When did you feel really 'listened to' today? What gave you that feeling? What impact did that level of listening have on you? What are you willing to change about your own listening to give that to others?

3) GIPP test time. Assess what generalizations, interpretations, personal experiences and preconceived notions (shaping assumptions and judgements) you have listen to others through today.

So we've explored a number of ways in which our listening filters may impact what we do with the information someone shares. How aware are you of your own GIPP?

Questions to play in:

When was the last time someone GIPP'd you versus taking you for who you are?

_____
_____
_____
_____
_____
_____
_____
_____

How did it make you feel? What was the impact on the situation?

_____
_____
_____
_____
_____
_____
_____
_____

What GIPP do you commonly place on others? Or when someone is listening to you, what GIPP filters do you assume they are seeing/ receiving you through?

_____
_____
_____
_____
_____
_____
_____
_____

How is your GIPP impacting your relationships?

_____

_____

_____

_____

_____

_____

_____

_____

What are you willing to change within yourself that will impact the intent of your listening?

_____

_____

_____

_____

_____

_____

_____

In additional to the three websites noted within the body of this text and End Noted, my insight on this topic has been enhanced from content experienced in my Coach training through both The Coaching Institute(9) and from CORE Consulting Inc.(10)

7

FULFILLMENT

Imagine your current life.

Mmhmm. Sit here for a minute and do the inventory of it.

Of what is your current life made up of? And if you feel stuck on how to answer this, another approach to this would be, in a 7-day week, what am I doing with my time?

_____

_____

_____

_____

_____

_____

_____

_____

_____

_____

_____

_____

_____

_____

_____

Now, consider your life again—and this time think about your future. What is your vision? What does it _LOOK_ like? What does it _FEEL_ like? What adjustments do you have to make to your current life to get to this? And yes, I'm anticipating some of your possible responses! Some of you are laughing thinking this is a ridiculous request. Others gasped in the thought of taking on such dramatic change. I dare you—write down whatever comes to your mind. Go for it.

_____

_____

_____

_____

_____

_____

_____

_____

_____

_____

_____

_____

_____

_____

_____

_____

So I ask you—is what you've written so dramatic? Is it so funny?

Let's play for a minute. My guess is you're approximately a third to half-way through your life. YOUR life. You've got a ton of learning under your belt, experiences that have shaped and moulded you to who you are today. Which of these experiences have you grown from? Which ones have you not fully experienced yet? And which ones are you ready to add to your life?

At a company I worked for when I was 24 years old my manager at the time sent an email to me acknowledging the work I had done for our shared client, and he carbon copied the VP of our organization. I saw my manager later that day in the hall and I thanked him for sending the email. He said "no problem but, don't count on me doing it again." His response surprised me so I asked "Have I done something wrong?". He said, "Not at all. Simply, the only person to take care of you is you. Next time someone needs to know about the job you're doing, you tell them." A great learning for me at a young age. Now I extend this learning to you.

The only person, no, let me rephrase that, the *number one* person who will take care of you is YOU. **What are you willing to do, to give yourself the life you want?**

I was facilitating a session yesterday for an International company. The company, although still doing well, needed to start doing better and part of this was promoting the leaders of the organization to step up and start leading at their level of capability. The leaders (majority had been employed at the company for a minimum of six years) were struggling with this role however because in the past, when they had been innovative, creative, strategic, forward-thinking and lead from within, they had been told to be compliant, follow company protocol, not to rock the company boat, etc. So although the leaders wanted to make change you could see the apprehension in their eyes and needed assurance from the president that they had his backing to do this. So I did two things.

1) We created and then tested the safety net: In front of the group I went through a series of questions with the president that allowed the leaders to hear the president basically confirm that not only did he have their back, he had their front and sides too. He enabled them to take charge, committed to supporting their decisions and they calibrated on what leadership and accountability meant for their individual roles.

2) We acknowledged their history for what it was . . . history (nothing more, nothing less): The leaders kept talking about the legacy at the company and how things had been done in the past. I asked if I could challenge them. With their agreement for the challenge I said, "We all have history. I like to call it a story. It makes us who we are. You can continue to live that history, that past, or you can simply let it be what it is, a piece of you (and in this situation, your company). You lived it and it helped developed you to this point. You can hold on to it tightly OR you can build on it like a foundation or platform to make you stronger. You've been given official permission to release yourself of the history that has held you back and have been given the security net that makes the risk(s) easier to make. So tell me this—are

you going to continue to let you/your company history hold you back like a ball and chain, or use it like springs under your feet to help you reach the heights you can be at? You're acting like this legacy is like a storm cloud overhead. You've been granted the power to move the cloud. BLOW IT AWAY and check out what that opens up for you."

The group didn't realise how much of an excuse AND impact this history had on them. It had gotten to the point that they were the ones making it repeat itself.

Hmmm . . . .

Yes. I'm looking right at you. And if you can't feel that, go get a mirror and stand in front of it. Do you continue to repeat your history—habits and patterns that aren't worth a second round. YOU own the ability to have anything you want. You may need support, resources, help, yet it's you, only you, who can take charge of getting and having what you want.

What are you going to do about getting what you want? Stick with the ball and chain situation (which is bringing little to your life) or allow your history to be exactly what it is, a part of you who makes you who you are today—grow from it and keep moving forward.

Oddly, the ball and chain may seem like the easier choice.

Do you know why?

Because that's what you know. Mmhmm. The new stuff is where we feel fear because it's the unknown. I challenge you to see and feel that sensation as excitement of living again, not fear. Anchor the energy of that sensation to propel you where you want to go.

IT'S PLANNING TIME:

Looking at what you came up with in your vision exercise on the previous page, what are you willing to give to yourself to have this more fulfilled life? Not finding you're coming up with anything? Then refer back to your

Wheel of Life exercise (chapter 4, page 21). What insights can you expand on from with that tool?

_____

_____

_____

_____

_____

_____

_____

What value(s) of yours does this chapter bring awareness to? And how important is it that you live these daily?

_____

_____

_____

_____

_____

_____

_____

What's your action plan to make this happen? AND don't be skimpy. You deserve it!

_____

_____

_____

_____

_____

_____

_____

By the way, while writing this I sense the 'I'll skip this section' vibe. Stick to this. I know it's tough. Anything new can be.

What will you risk by not doing this for yourself? What will you lose?

8

WOWs and WANTs

I wonder if you set annual objectives for yourself. Some might look at this as goal setting and others may consider these New Year's Resolutions. Some create resolutions & reach them. Some people use the same one from last year creating the "never quite reach it" syndrome. And some skip the annual goal setting/ New Year Resolution process all together.

Me—I'm not a New Year Resolution gal. Instead—I focus on WOWs & WANTs. Every December 31ˢᵗ I make the time to sit with a pen & paper and reflect. I start by recording the WOWs I've had from the current year. I record them for all aspects of my life (career, financial situation, family, friends, health, dating-ships, fun, community, travel, etc). It's a great list to create—a terrific reminder of what's important to me & what I've pulled off. Then I flip the page over, record the date and then list what my WANTs are for the upcoming year. Again—a great reach for me, keeping me away from 'functioning' in my life and focusing on living it. I've done this for 3 years now. After the first year, I created a file folder that I store this annual list in. I pull out the list from the previous year and compare the WANTs from the year prior with the WOWs from the list I just created.

This process means a lot to me. It's a touchstone for connecting to my values and it's a warm way to capture the year at a glance and allow me to see what I have done for me to have the life that I want. This past year I decided it was time to 'one up' the WOWs and WANTs list so I added two additional components.

The first component was ownership. It was terrific to record a list of WANTs in my life yet, what was that leaving me with from a directional stand point? So I sat with my WOWs and WANTs folder and reviewed my three WOWs lists to see what, if any, commonalities I could find. For example, was I leaning more to activity-based wins or physical environment/ home renovation changes? And more importantly to me, what areas did I seem low in or was skipping all together and was what the reason. I captured some notes and was ready for Step Three. Flipping the sheets over to the WANTs side of the page I looked for any repeated themes from the past three years. I was looking for areas I really wanted more in or areas that were noted yet that I was not getting traction with. Again, I captured some objective observations on my notes page and was ready for Step Four.

Quick Recap:

Step 1—Create WOWs list
Step 2—Create WANTs list
Step 3—Review lists from steps 1 & 2 and assess

Step is the appropriate word here. Each year I have noted this as important to myself, yet somehow I hadn't allowed myself the time I need to address it. Let me make sure this is clear to you: you don't need a list for this. I have shared my WOWs and WANTs list making program because I love the reflection experience it gives me and if you decide to do it for yourself, fantastic. Take it on today & make this your annual date in your calendar. However, I believe this WOWs and WANTs list lives inside us and many people simply haven't trapped it to paper. So an excuse like 'well I don't have a list so I'm going to skip this part' isn't going to fly with me. You have the list. It's in your heart and your head. Jump the barrier with me and let's make this happen for you.

Okay, back to Step Four.

Using the Wheel of Life format from Chapter four called What's your Ride Like?, I drew a circle on a large piece of paper (11 by 14). With coloured markers I cut the circle into triangular, pie shapes. Then, I considered the areas that stood out to me and bucketed them under headings i.e. Career. I prioritized these items and then using the coloured markers labeled the Wheel pieces with these bucket names. Once I had 8 labels, I went back to my note list and challenged myself on both creating and capturing steps, with timing, for each of these WANTs.

Pause. Once that's completed, you have an opportunity. For those of you who have significant others or children, you have an opportunity to bring everyone into the huddle and into the game which brings us to Step Five.

I have two great, energetic boys for whom I work to create an environment to live in that includes discussing about giving, charity, values and life. At their ages I thought creating awareness about each other's WANTs and how to get there would be a valuable discussion. I wanted to explore what we might potentially create as a family to complete and also how we could support each other getting to any achieved WANTs. I had no idea how this was going to go, let alone if they'd sit down long enough to listen to my idea. Then, smartly, I reminded myself that anything was a start & not worry about it.

In preparation I had a couple pieces of 11 x14 paper with one large circle on each, and divided each circle by 8. With coloured markers, I called the boys to the kitchen table. As you can imagine, communication is important in our home. The boys understand a fair amount about my business and I share things like when I get new clients and contracts, how my success impacts what we do, etc. With that platform already paved, that's how I started our meeting. My introduction went something like this: *Boys, you know how with Life Dots I have a clear plan and goals to reach to be able to build my business so then we can have the money and time to do the family stuff we want to do? For me to create these goals I give some thought to what I WANT my year to look like, and then I capture it in a wheel like this. I want us to create a 'Wheel of WANTs' for our family for this year. To get started we need to agree to what's important to us so shout out different things that are important to you, and using these different coloured markers I am going to note them on our circle pieces.*

And that's how easy it was. We together created our topic buckets agreeing to focus on community, school/ career, money, family, personal growth, health (food), health (activity), and home. Under each section we colour coded the WANT based on who the goal is for. Some apply to all three of us, and some our individual. A couple WOWs for me came out of the experience:

- My son's goal is to 'have peace' in our home (meaning no yelling). Imagine how many times I will reference that this year!
- They made report card goals, chore jar financial goals and tripled how they want to give back to our community. Without my coaxing. Ha—skip WOWs, how about SUPER WOWs!
- They learned about my goals and why I am focusing on what I am. Without this conversation today, I might not have shared this simply because it might not have seemed important.
- They asked to make a second chart, specific to saving money!

This chart now hangs in our kitchen, beside our meal table. It's referenced at least weekly. Not only is it a touchstone for me, it is for the boys as well. We don't know about a situation unless we apply it and really try it on. Imagine if you learned how to set goals when you were 6 or 8 years of age. Wonder where you'd be with your Resolutions today?

Family rocks. Create yours. Make yours what you want it to be. This exercise gave me a glimpse of what my boys want it to be. Lucky me. Now I can support them in reaching their goals and they can follow and support me with mine.

Now it's your turn, application time.

First—I suggested four individual steps. They are:

Step 1—Create your list of WOWs.
Step 2—Create your list of WANTs.
Step 3—Critique your own lists, objectively, and find what's there for you as personal opportunity.
Step 4—Create your WANTs Wheel of Action.
Optional Step 5—Create a WANTs Wheel of Action with your family.

The next four pages provide you the template to capture this.

Go to http://lifedots.ca/connect-with-your-dots-template/ for larger printable worksheets.

Step 1: Create your past year WOWs. Cover all areas within your life. Some of these may be career, family, friends, significant other, health, fun and recreation, money, community, personal growth, home. Consider anything that is different from the year prior.

_____

_____

_____

_____

_____

_____

_____

_____

_____

_____

_____

_____

_____

_____

_____

_____

_____

_____

_____

_____

_____

_____

_____

_____

_____

_____

_____

_____

_____

_____

_____

_____

Step 2: Create your upcoming year of WANTs again covering all areas within your life like you did for your WOWs in Step One.

_____

_____

_____

_____

_____

_____

_____

_____

_____

_____

_____

_____

_____

_____

_____

_____

_____

_____

_____

_____

_____

_____

_____

_____

_____

_____

_____

_____

_____

_____

_____

_____

_____

_____

_____

_____

_____

Step 3: Reviewing your list of WOWs and WANTs, using a separate piece of paper, note your observations. What patterns are you seeing? What areas are you skipping over? Which areas feel super saturated?

_____

_____

_____

_____

_____

_____

_____

_____

_____

_____

_____

_____

_____

_____

_____

_____

_____

_____

_____

_____

_____

_____

_____

_____

_____

_____

_____

_____

_____

_____

_____

_____

_____

_____

Step 4: Using your Step Three findings, Create your wheel of WANTs steps. Be specific, include timing, be realistic and have fun. *I have started you with four areas to focus on. Add more to suit your need.*

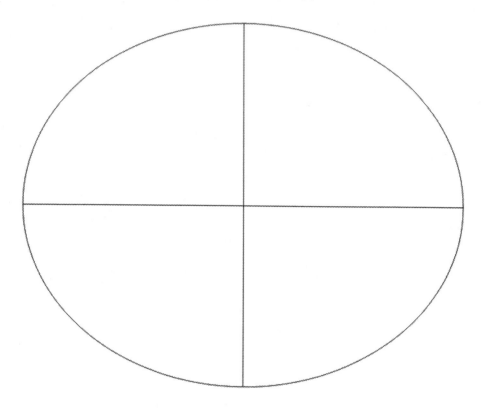

Step 5: Family huddle time. Reread the script I provided and decide on your approach with your family.

Pull what you need together (markers, flip chart paper, incentive treats, etc)

Create your family Wheels of Action.

Colour code based on whose action it is.

Be specific, include timing, be realistic and have fun.

I have started you with four areas to focus on. Add more to suit your need.

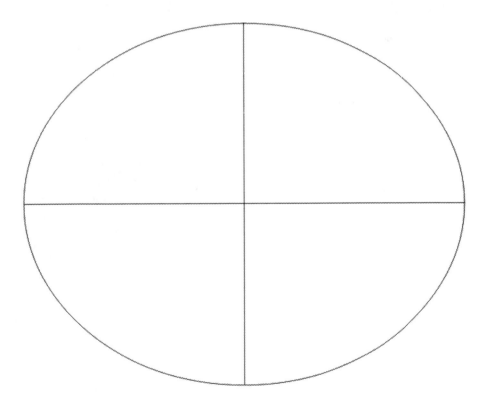

9

BE WITH

Ever have something in your life happen that set you off your track? Something that you didn't realise set you off your track. Or maybe you did realise it, yet left the experience to sit inside you, unresolved.

One of mine was sex. Yep. I lost my virginity when I was too young. That's my opinion, not enforced by parents or others. I thought I was going to be married a virgin. Stop laughing, I'm serious. I thought that's how 'it' worked. I thought that was the only option. You married and then babies came. Clearly I wasn't the strongest Sex Education student Richview Collegiate had ever encountered. We don't need to get into the sex part of it so simply—I wasn't raped, I don't blame the guy, nor do I blame myself. I was young and I didn't have the self-awareness or esteem to stand up for myself and what was important to me. Remember that GIPP thing a couple chapters back? Well, this was my negative judgement on the situation. Self-inflicted.

So. Not a "horrific" example or a "tragic" example. It is however an example that has had a lot of impact on me. And it stumped me for a long time. I had spoken to a psychologist about it and close friends and past partners know about it. I've always been open about it, spoken easily about it and shared the story when I felt I needed to talk about it, get deeper with it or shake it out of my head.

Interesting, I had the relatively-recent realization that I had only spoken about it from my head. Not my heart. I've acknowledged the situation again and again and again, you get my point . . . But what I hadn't done was really "been with" it.

What does *be with it* mean? Different things to different people would be my guess. And *be with* would also be different for any situation.

Specific to my example, I needed to *be with* the emotion of mourning the loss of something that was important to me, of not taking a stand for something I valued and that mattered to me. I needed to acknowledge (and finally feel) the pain of all those years ago to be able to get through it.

TA-DA! Connection. I had to be with it holistically, not just with one part of me. In this example I had only been with it with my head. Not my heart.

Another example, my divorce from my husband. I initiated the separation and there's not a cell in my body that believes I made the wrong decision. My children now have better lives and the mother they deserve—fully present, more relaxed, calm, happy, consistent, etc. Here's the catch; to get through to the other side of separation, I needed to *be with* and release the emotion of taking our precious boys out of our society's traditional view of a family and home. I needed to *be with* the guilt of my children having to grow up having parents under separate roofs and find a neutrality with nights that "it's not my turn" to be with them. I understood and could easily speak with others about it (again, being with it in my head) but I had to take the time for myself in my heart and spirit to connect with and release the pain/grieve/fear/sadness of having children not with me, the way I believed they should be.

When I meet with coaching clients, I describe *be with* like a block in your blood vessel. Visualise this with me. Picture a rough black stone within your vein, semi-blocking your blood flow. Your blood is able to get around this stone, but the stone is blocking the speed and flow of your blood to your heart, which impacts how well your heart can pump. You can function like this sure, yet instead imagine yourself spending the time to sand that stone down, so more blood can get through; releasing the pressure on your heart, allowing your blood to move more consistently through your body. Imagine the change in your energy level, no longer clogged by this "not being with" black stone. Appreciate the difference in your daily function—your steps being lighter, your pace being rhythmic, your focus being on 'the good stuff' again. Imagine that stone being sanded to dust, carried out of your life forever.

GIPP sucks, we already established that. Some other stuff sucks too. The top of my list would include guilt, life blocks, barriers or experiences we don't grow from and the inconsistency of my fridge compressor thus breaking down again and again (it's a personal list . . . you get to make your own in a moment). What we all need to remember though: We choose. We choose to play or pass, we choose to hold onto stuff or other people's stuff and/or make it our own stuff. We choose to hold tight to the black stones in our blood vessels or to sand them in to dust and clear them of our body forever. What do you choose?

Remember the Wheel of Life exercise from Chapter Four "What's your Ride like?" that outlined the different areas of your life. Using this as a tool, what comes up in any of the areas for you as something that you need to fully *be with*?

_____

_____

_____

_____

_____

_____

_____

_____

What do you need to allow yourself to *be with* it? What's blocking you?

_____

_____

_____

_____

_____

_____

_____

_____

How do you know it's time to let this go?

Please don't skip this question. I believe your answer may both help you free your "black stone" and give you the ownership you need to do this for yourself.

_____
_____
_____
_____
_____
_____
_____
_____

What do you need to do this?

_____
_____
_____
_____
_____
_____
_____

Insert deep breath here.

And what will you commit to yourself right now, to make this happen?

_____
_____
_____
_____
_____
_____

Do this for you. You deserve it.

10

EARPLUGS

I am laughing as I write this! So . . . in the last year of my marriage I started wearing earplugs to sleep. And it made the difference between a scattered night of "naps" to a full night's sleep.

What's funny to me about this now is what in reflection the earplugs represent to me! What were the earplugs shutting out (letting me sleep peacefully) and why don't I need them anymore?! What sanity did the earplugs provide me? What barrier did they create to 'save me' from? Amusing to me now, how little I realised this at the time.

A client I'm working with currently uses "I don't know, what do you think?" when we are coaching. She does this often enough that it became one of her coaching session agenda topics. She realised that through some tough childhood experiences she was taught that her opinions and thoughts didn't matter, to the point there is scarring. Her trained automatic response when asked for an answer is "I don't know what do you think?". In my opinion that's a plug. It's a boundary set by a life experience that is causing this individual to not be true to herself and to 'camouflage" the hole created by a not-good situation.

What plugs are you currently using in your life? Commonly, people use work (by overworking) and food (by overeating). What's yours? Let's take some time here—because my guess is that you're prepared to keep reading without answering the question. What's your plug?

Need clarity? What are you using currently to block you from some of life realisations? What's your crutch to get through whatever it is that's tough to handle right now?

I like this term plug. To me it represents something we use to block a hole, the hole being something that's missing. I think others may see it as a space holder and others as a "welcomed" filter. Try those three perspectives on for your plug. Is it a block (holding you back from moving forward with something), a space holder (you crave something but feel you can't have it, or that it is unattainable so instead use this plug as a surrogate or runner-up) or is it a welcome filter (the thing that's keeping you sane through all the other crap—like an outlet!). Which perspective are you currently 'plugging'? And what are you losing by using it?

Seeing some similarities with the last chapter about to *be with* something? Handy to have them back to back isn't it. They definitely have their similarities. They also have their differences. To *be with* perspective is more like a rug that you use to cover up something you haven't dealt with. The plug is the block or barrier that holds you from the energy and the potential of being more of you. Don't let yourself off the hook on this one. What's your plug?

What are your plugs/space holders/welcome filters?

_____
_____
_____
_____
_____
_____
_____
_____

What false security are they giving you? Yes, it is a great question.

_____
_____
_____
_____
_____
_____
_____
_____

What are you specifically losing from your life by avoiding dealing with reason for the plug directly?

_____

_____

_____

_____

_____

_____

_____

_____

What makes it worth holding onto?

_____

_____

_____

_____

_____

_____

_____

Nothing (in my opinion).

And you know what's coming . . . What's your decision: keep the plug or remove the plug from your life forever. Circle your choice:

REMOVE PLUG   keep plug

Now, time to own it. What's your action plan to remove this plug. Write it out. The specific what's & how's to make it happen, the timing and who you need to involve. And please, if this format doesn't work for you, fetch a piece of paper and create a format that will.

the What   the How   your Timing   What support you need
                                          to make it happen?

_____
_____
_____
_____
_____
_____
_____
_____
_____
_____
_____
_____
_____
_____
_____
_____
_____
_____
_____
_____
_____
_____
_____

11

PARAMETERS

When participating in my CTI coaching course, one of the first tools I was introduced to was called *designing an alliance.* (12) We participants were taught that any time we were to start a new relationship with a coaching client, before we could move forward with any coaching, we needed to first design an alliance with them. Other words for alliance include pact, agreement, and deal. I have a client in Georgia who calls it our Communication Agreement. Call it what you want. Alliance is what I (currently) call it so for the purpose of this chapter, alliance it is. This alliance allows both the coach and the client to voice any specific needs they required of each other. Some things that may be talked through in this discussion may include:

- Confidentiality
- Willingness to being open to new ideas and perspective
- Discussing what each other needs to create a safe/trusting environment in which one can be vulnerable, truly vulnerable to have the journey required to get what they want
- Agreeing that we can push/challenge each other if we believe the other has more to give/do. And in the same breathe say "hold up, that's too much. No."
- If anything is not working in the coaching relationship either of us will acknowledge it in the moment and discuss what need to happen to change it
- Interrupting
- Use of profanity
- Ease of being direct
- Ongoing opportunity to adjust relationship to the need, as needed

This alliance is considered a starting point for the coaching relationship. Then, once the actual coaching begins, at any point either the coach or client may ask to adjust or make amendments to the original agreed to alliance. Pretty straight forward. A designed alliance between a coach and a client defines the parameters of the relationship based off both people's wants and needs.

Smart idea.

The Monday after my weekend session, I went back to the workplace. I was facilitating a training session for 30 employees at a consumer packaged goods company and clearly, a number of the participants were prisoners (told they 'must' attend the session) and vacationers (signed up for the course for a 'day off' their desk job) versus fully fledged, "I'm interested in learning more about the training topic and refining my skills" participants. Sometimes this happens in companies. So I was couple minutes into my 'standard' introduction and I stopped mid-sentence. I explained about this new-to-me designed alliance concept and asked if they were willing to create one with me. Then as a group, based on their needs (and mine) we redesigned the working space for our session. This required moving the furniture around to create a more comfortable and welcoming working environment, tweaking the content to more specifically meet the learners needs and hourly blackberry breaks of 5 minutes versus a 15 minute break every 3 hours. On my end I asked for them to be fully present in the session and did an exercise with them to help 'clear' the other stuff from their mind so they could do that. I also asked for them to actively participate and asked for permission to call them out on it if they weren't engaged.

So the session went from "it should go alright" to "the facilitator and participants are committed to making this training as productive and engaging as possible for all". What a difference. And that was confirmed for me both in the active participation throughout the day as well as the feedback I received after the session.

Later that week, I was at a monthly meeting with five other coaches that are also friends of mine. When we were giving personal updates to each other I shared the alliance experience in the training room that I just shared with you. Then I moved on to my personal life with my dating update. One coach clearly saw the resonance when I was speaking about this guy I was dating and called me out on it. Then she says "Will you accept the challenge of designing an alliance with him?" "Yikes" said one of my inner voices. Another inner voice said "Darn straight I will". So I took the challenge! And I did it.

First I needed to be clear with myself with what I wanted from the relationship. Here's the list I came up with including how I defined it to him, in brackets. I was cognizant of how easily we could interpret the meaning of something so gosh darn it, if I was going to take this alliance on, it was going to be clear!

- Open communication (that included no holding back, complete honesty and active listening with no hidden agendas)
- Being fully present (if either of us were finding that the relationship was no longer working for us we were to 'call it' and explain why versus slowly withdrawing from the situation)
- Taking risks/being vulnerable (for me this included asking whatever I wanted to learn more about and trusting that when he asked me similar questions I could answer fully without being judged for my response)
- Fun/Aliveness (Life is short! If the fun factor starts to waiver—either has to call the other on it)

Then, that night on the phone I introduced the alliance concept and asked him if he was game (and yes, I did feel a bit awkward but, seriously—I had nothing to lose here so what the heck!). He said sure. So I asked him what he need from me. After we agreed to his list, we went through mine. It was a great exploration of understanding each other from a wants, needs and values standpoint.

For Level One Listening interest sake—the relationship went and additional three months after this conversation. Yep, 12 weeks. And although that may seem really short to you reading this, it was one of the best relationships I had been in up to that point in my life. We laughed a lot, our communication was crystal and I learned a ton about my personal needs as well as my relationship needs. At the end of it, probably because of both the alliance exercise and my own self-awareness, we (ok "I", but it was then openly discussed) identified the 'something' that was missing for me as something he couldn't naturally deliver. It was the healthiest break-up I have ever had. And I'm proud of it because I stayed true to myself and my needs throughout the relationship. We had created parameters for our relationship so it could have everything it needed to grow fully. We fully committed to trying it out and both left the relationship unscathed. And I left knowing that there's 'a better match' for me.

Confession: Old habits die hard. I waivered. YES—for those of you saying "silly girl!" you are right. My gut knew yet, the want in my heart hoped for more. So after this initial break-up, we toiled through another five weeks of uneven give and take stuff. Then I ended it again. Lessons learned by me include:

- (again) Your gut is there for a reason. *Listen to it!*
- Designed alliances are there for a reason. *Use them properly and fully!*
- For a gal who hadn't dated for 11 years I did a pretty good job of taking care of me in this round!

Since that break up, every relationship I have been in we've created an alliance, accept for one. And that one break up left me on my butt for a while . . . We all need clarity. Honesty and transparency is welcome in any time of relationship. Games have rules, businesses have policies, and DVD players have instruction manuals. Relationships with alliances can be WOWIE. I personally think we all deserve WOWIE.

I've illustrated the alliance use in working relationships (both one-on-one and groups) and significant other relationships. I now use alliances in a variety of relationships you would easily identify through linking people to using the Wheel of Live (Chapter Four, What's your Ride Like?). Friendships, family-ships, my cleaning lady, two individuals whom 'have to' be in my life that I felt I needed to set parameters with to allow me to deal with the 'obligations' of those relationships. Alliances are a great platform to build any type of 'ship on. Imagine having transparency with people, clarity on your needs and theirs, and agreed to ways to acknowledge when you're not getting what you need. Again, WOWIE.

Now it's your turn. Think about the various relationships in your life. Friendships, family-ships, work-ships, partnerships, work colleagues, consistent meeting groups. Which ones have become compliant? Which ones need an update or an overhaul? Which ones deserve a review? Choose three and spend the time understanding what you need for each of one of them to be the relationship you want to be.

TIME TO CREATE/REVIVE SOME OF YOUR ALLIANCES:

Relationship #1: _____

What I need in the alliance:

_____
_____
_____
_____
_____
_____
_____

When will you have this conversation?

_____

What will you lose if you don't?

_____
_____
_____
_____
_____
_____
_____

Relationship #2: _____

What I need in the alliance:

_____

_____

_____

_____

_____

_____

_____

When will you have this conversation?

_____

What will you lose if you don't?

_____

_____

_____

_____

_____

_____

_____

Relationship #3: _____

What I need in the alliance:

_____

_____

_____

_____

_____

_____

_____

When will you have this conversation?

_____

What will you lose if you don't?

_____
_____
_____
_____
_____
_____
_____

COUPLE ADDITIONAL FOLLOW UP QUESTIONS FOR YOU:

What did you learn for yourself when you went through the experience of setting up these alliances?

_____
_____
_____
_____
_____
_____
_____

What will you now do differently in all your relationships?

_____
_____
_____
_____
_____
_____
_____

12

CONNECTED LIFE DOTS

Ever been thinking about someone and the phone then rings hosting that person on the other end of the connection? Or thought, "wouldn't it be great if . . ." and then it actually happened. I, like most of us, have had that happen from time-to-time in my life.

And then something happened.

Without assuming this has been clear from your reading so far, I've made some recent life changes. I have undertaken a journey to reclaim myself. Sounds a tad dramatic yet, typing it felt good. So good in fact I'm going to say it again. Reclaim myself. Yep, feels just as good the second time.

The ending of my eight-year marriage played a huge role in reclaiming me. Once I realised the 'spot' I/my life/my family was in and took the accountability for the role I played in creating it AND the responsibility I have to both myself and my children to change this, things began to happen. Best way for me to describe it brings me to a visual. Picture this giant hand holding on to all the puzzle pieces of my life. The giant hand shakes them like a pair of die and throws them to the air. This shake up allows the pieces to disconnect from their originally found spot, and relocate to another place when then land. So . . . my life pieces are MY pieces. I needed to play the primary role to see how they fit in my life puzzle, my way.

When you become the giant for yourself, the one who can control your choices and align with your wants, not only do you start living a better, richer life, you align yourself with natural coincidental occurrence because you're where you're supposed to be. I like the visual of the giant because sometimes we can feel like we have little to no control of things in our lives, feeling opposite of a giant in our lives. The giant to me is the reminder of the role I am suppose to play in my life. It is my life to have.

Some people talk about when 'stars align'. Others call it coincidental occurrence. Before April 2009, I thought 'that's nice' when other people referenced this happening for them. It was something I wasn't really aware of or a big believer in. Then, when I started my own self-exploration on what the heck I was both doing in my life and wanting in my life, I saw it as 'connecting my life dots'. For a point of reference, the Wheel of Life segments (health, career, physical environment, etc) are what I see as my Life Dots. When I am at my best and being the giant in my life (yes, that's right, when I am in my *Happy Place*), my Life Dots connect, literally—keeping me whole, balanced, in place. When I now stray from what is the best choice for me and therefore no longer connecting to my core values, the dots misalign and things fall. To recap:

Stay connected with my values = great things keep happening.

Lose focus on the right stuff = misalignment of dots; things aren't as rosy as they could be

Let me give you an example. When I am functioning in what I like to call "my wow" (it's a good spot to be), the dots align a number of times a day. If I'm feeling a bit crunched for time, a client will call with an apology of running late, and reschedule for next week. Or if I'd prefer an early time for an appointment, the office the appointment is held with calls because they had a last-minute cancellation. Or, like this afternoon, as I am sitting at the shoreline writing this chapter, basking in the sunshine of a beautiful autumn day, listening to the waves hit the shore, this amazing guitar player springs out of nowhere and starts playing music that I couldn't have requested to be any more fitting. I KNOW—I can't believe it either! Marvellously, this now happens to me. A lot. Coincidental Occurrence. Dreamy isn't it.

Now, here's the great flip side to it. When things go *the other way*, I now respond differently. Instead of woe-as-me, I sit in it. "What's the learning here? What's the bigger thing within this situation that I'm supposed to be understanding?" Let me share an example.

I received an email from a company for which I do both facilitation and coaching work. They were wondering if I'd be available for a multi-day gig in Italy . . . in 3 weeks time. Let me restate that: ITALY! "Darn straight I'm available!" So, I then proceed to jump through and over hoops to make this happen—change my schedule, set up an insane amount of child support, borrow CDs from the library to start learning the language, etc. I am pumped! I've never been to Europe before. And it's going to happen in three and a half weeks—WaHOOOOO! My guess is that you know what's coming. Yep. Italy got cancelled, 7 days after it was offered. And yes, wind dropped from my sail faster than a blink of an eye. BUT, not for long. I reassessed the situation: "what's in here for me to learn about?" . . . A couple biggies:

1) Europe. I'm clearly keen to get there. The number one place I'd like to see is Greece, number two is Italy. If it's that exciting for me, make it happen! Result: I have booked a trip. A week long bike tour of Croatia followed by a week in Italy. I have also vowed to take an annual trip to somewhere 'WOW'. You live once, make it happen.

2) Hold tight to your parameters. Past experiences with this company made me realise I needed to redesign my alliance with this company, to review my needs of them and confirm theirs of me.

3) Take care of yourself. No one else will do it for you (remember what I said about the giant earlier). My contract cancellation clause did not capture this lost revenue. If my clause then was where it is now, my recently booked Croatia bike trip costs would have been paid for and then some. Lesson learned.

Sometimes people say "things happening for a reason". This used to just be a saying to me. Now, I can reflect on certain things (yes, I know, hindsight is 20/20) and think hmm . . . here's how many times I missed learning this lesson. I love the learning part. I just want to stop the getting hit over the head with it! So I work hard to stay connected to my life values and to BE in more life moments then getting caught in the "doing" within the moments. When I'm connected this way, life is good. Really, really good. Fortunately, I've had enough of a taste of this side of the connected Life Dots that I want to stay here. It motivates me to work to stay on this side. Life is short . . . BE more.

QUESTIONS FOR YOU TO PLAY IN:

When you read about connecting <u>your</u> Life Dots, what was the first thought that came to your mind?

_____

_____

_____

_____

_____

_____

_____

_____

What's getting in the way of you connecting with what you really want to be doing in your life?

_____

_____

_____

_____

_____

_____

_____

_____

Specific to your answer above, how long have you known, and what has 'not doing anything about it' given you/your life to date?

_____
_____
_____
_____
_____
_____
_____
_____

What will make you change this for yourself?

_____
_____
_____
_____
_____
_____
_____
_____

Who will you ask for the help /support/resources to let you get what you want?

_____
_____
_____
_____
_____
_____
_____
_____

WHEN?! What will make you start this today?

_____

_____

_____

_____

_____

_____

_____

_____

QUALITY ASSURANCE CHECK

Here we are. The half way point.

In the "how to use this book' section, I suggested keeping your reading and exercise chunks to 45 minute sessions to allow you insight & reflection time and also providing you the time needed to go implement what you said you were going to do. So . . . how's it coming?

As a coach, a rule I was taught was the 10-80-10 rule. The first 10% is coaching on the actual situation, the 80% is the exploring of the topic (and linking this exploration to important topics, values, future wants, etc of the client's) followed by the remaining 10% which is the what you will do next to make it happen, be with it, deal with it, etc. After the exploration (the digging deeper) with the client, the final 10% is about committing to what needs to happen for the client to have what they want. An agreement to what they are going to do, the specifics to that agreement, the timeline AND apply a touchstone for them to ensure they stay on track.Clients have different touchstones—for example; some clients send me a weekly progress update, one current client sends me a one line "I'm doing it" daily email, and recently a client of mine said she'd keep herself accountable & if she didn't adhere to it, she would pay me double the next session. Quite the penalty yet, held her to completion. What's holding you to the completion of your action plans in this book & getting the life you want? And are you spending the 80% of exploration time required to dig to the root of your thoughts and feelings on the various topics we have uncovered in this process so far?

If you have completed the action plans you have created for the first 11 chapters, CONGRATULATIONS! Go celebrate yourself in any way you see fit. YOU and your milestones deserve celebration. Ta-Da! (And, skip ahead to topic 12.)

For those of you who haven't completed them . . . . what's going on?

Is there a *plug*? Something you won't *be with*? Too many *shoulds* in the way of your *Must-Ticks*?

I know you know you are worth it because you are reading this book. However, by not completing the exercises and action plans, all this experience will be is "just another book I bought & read a portion of before it joined 'the others' in my ever expanding self-help library."

So . . . a couple ideas:

1. Go back to the start and flip through chapters 1 through 11. Fold down the pages you still need to spend time on. Then put the book down for 7 days. Come back and take the questions one topic at a time.
2. Review how you are setting up your action plan. When working with clients we ensure that our action plan is well outlined. The acronym we follow is S.M.A.R.T. In business they often say S.M.A.R.T stands for: Specific, Measurable, Actionable, Realistic and Timely. (11) Through my coach training CTI taught me S.M.A.R.T stands for: Specific, Measurable, Accountable, Resonant and Thrilling. If creating an action plan detailed enough to put you into action is a block for you, please go to Appendix A for my personal example to help you along.
3. Feeling stuck & need more assistance getting where you want to go? Ask for help. This is what the Coaching industry is all about. Get a reputable, certified coach. Not sure where to start? My recommendation is The Coaches Training Institute http://www.coactivenetwork.com/webx?ctiFindACoach. Coaching can be done anywhere and suited to your schedule. I have had both International and local clients. Coaching can be done many ways including face-to-face, over the phone or via Skype. Try a couple

coaches before you commit to one. Ask for a sample session to ensure you both think it's a match. And if my style is working for you, contact me Nancy@lifedots.ca and if I'm not a fit, I've got lots of coaching colleagues to refer you to based on your need and style.

4. Persevere. You didn't create your 'tough stuff' in a few hours—it's built up over time. Give yourself permission to take your time through it YET be diligent and stick with it. There's a term for it. Baby steps. And this process is about both the journey and the results.

5. Screw excuses. Have you noticed that I haven't asked you 'why' in any of the exercise questions? Often coaches don't ask why. Why can allow the person being asked the opportunity to story tell, give excuses, opinions and can put people on the defensive. Sticking with 'what' & 'how' questions will keep you out of the excuse merry-go-round and make you stick with the realities of the situation.

I won't ask you what excuses you are making for not answering your questions. What I will do is ask you this: How are you excuses impacting your life?

Important to note, the exploration is where so much of the 'stuff' is. The 80% of time I referred to earlier. There is value in the feeling of discomfort. Push yourself further than you usual go and see what you find 'in there'.

The journey through this book can bring you results. If you don't fully participate in the journey, you'll end up relatively close to the same spot you started. That would suck.

It's time. Own it. Own the process. Own your life. You only get one.

13

WHAT ARE YOU GOING TO MAKE OF IT?

A recent experience has made me think about how we as individuals take care of ourselves. Often, through past experiences we create habits and behaviours to either recreate similar experiences or to do the reverse, keep us from creating those experiences again.

For example, years ago I was renting the second-floor apartment of a house. It was a lovely old home that had been divided into a bunch of different-sized, oddly-shaped apartments. When I moved in they were still adding a balcony off my kitchen —just large enough to host 2 chairs and a BBQ. (Which was fortunate because I bought my BBQ before my bed . . . clearly my dinner intake was the priority). Long story short, while gabbing on a friend's voicemail, I went out to the still-no-railing-attached balcony to light the BBQ, and the industrial strength, fire proof kitchen door slams shut behind me. I laughed into the voicemail message—"Ha, hope that door didn't lock". One guess what happened . . . yep, I was locked on the balcony with no railing, with quickly growing nerves on how I was going to get down. I'm eyeing trees, looking for lattice to substitute for a ladder and cursing myself for my multi tasking obsession . . . I was out there for over 30 minutes. Minor, yes. At the time, I was shaky and freaked; I sway when it comes to height stuff. Oddly, I can tandem skydive because the guy attached to my back has been trained to get me to safety yet, a balcony ledge on my own . . . eek! Handy that I had the phone, and pleased with myself that I didn't call the fire department to get me down like a cat in a tree! I called a 'lives in the neighbourhood' girlfriend number repeatedly and once I reached her, she came and saved my day. My BBQ /Kitchen door lesson: triple check the door is unlocked and shove ANYTHING possible in the door to ensure the door can't close. EVER. In the 3 years I lived there, it didn't happen again. In addition I now have a "thing" with doors . . . I double check if all doors are locked when I am leaving my house and when going to bed at night. And I always double check if the garage door is closed, often reversing on the street for a triple check. I'm not even going to get into my car door being locked obsession with you!

On the other end, a CRAZY story for you. While 6 months pregnant with my second child, my husband-at-the-time and I travelled to Dominican Republic. The resort we are staying at was huge, one that spreads over acres of land and hosts 16 rooms in two-story villa setups with restaurants and pools sprinkled in between. When we checked into the resort, my one-year-old son was overdue for a nap so we took the only room available at the time, on the first floor (my rule of thumb with travel is to never be on the first floor of a hotel—from a break-in/ safety perspective). My husband was "Mr. Safety"—a name he earned easily due to the cautions he would watch for and his actions in situations. Specific to this trip, he packed an entire kit of medications for all of us in case of ANYTHING, and covered my son's hotel crib in netting in protection of bug bites. So . . . two days into the vacation, we are back in the hotel room after a great day at the beach. I'm in the shower and my former husband starts screaming 'Nancy GET OUT OF THE SHOWER! NOW!" I've got shampoo in my hair and I'm thinking to myself . . . "ok, what's happened to my son . . . maybe a bug bite, ho hum." He comes running in, shoves our son into my arms and says "Shots have been fired, I've seen bloody men, and it's chaos outside. STAY DOWN and keep the baby quiet!" The only thing separating us from the situation is the sliding glass door. Did I mention we were in a five-star hotel?!

So, covered in soap and shampoo, I put on my only clothing available in the bathroom (my sweaty workout clothes) and climb underneath the bathroom sink with my baby, singing sweet songs in his ear as I attempt to portray "we're ok" while internally I'm fearing the unknown and concerned that I'm going to miscarry my 2nd child. At one point men were running through the hallways of our unit, banging on the hotel room doors, yelling in a different language, trying to get access to the various hotel rooms, including ours. Insane thoughts are going through my head of men breaking through our locked door and killing us and taking my son. The two men staying in the hotel room above us grab their passports and ran. No shoes—just shorts and passports—one with shaving cream on half his face. Thirty minutes later, while my former husband on his hands and knees has packed our suitcases and I've used the phone in the bathroom for the series of "HELP US" calls to the hotel reception area, help arrives and we are escorted through blood-trailed footprints to a car taking us to safety. We were then relocated to a room on the other side of the hotel.

So what had happened? They were building a new hotel beside the one we were staying at. Busy season was quickly approaching and the hotel was to be finished by the end of the month yet, was behind. The soon-to-be hotel owners brought Haitian workers in to work with the Dominican workers. A fight broke out between them, and one of the workers used a machete on another. This caused group chaos and the security guard, seeing this, shot his gun in the air attempting to get all to disperse yet instead, it created a riot like response. It was quite the event for us. My husband called our travel agent from the new hotel room begging to get us on the next flight out. He broke down on the call—me taking the phone from his hand to finish the conversation with the agent. It's one of the three times I ever saw him cry. He vowed then and there that he'd never be back to Dominican Republic. The agent wasn't able to get us a flight out so instead we received a fruit basket for 10 people (amusing to me as we were at an all-inclusive resort), free services at the spa and a partial reimbursement for the trip.

Why am I sharing this story? Ironically, I'm completely fine with going back to the Dominican. Yes—it was a CRAZY, scary experience yet, it a total fluke experience. There were 1200 other resort guests who knew nothing of this isolated incident. The hotel staff were unfazed by the situation (they were born and raised in the country and have a book-load of scary experiences they could share I am sure) and compensated us more than any of the other guests because of how visibly pregnant I was and the concern of harm for my unborn baby.

So how is it I am now obsessed with door locks yet, have no problem with Dominican travel? I think it's both what and how I decided to deal with the situation. With the door situation I took on the perspective of 'that's not going to happen to me again' where is with the machete scare in Dominican I chalked it up to 'it is what it is, move on'.

Cookoo? Maybe. Yet we all do it.

Think about how life-limiting the one approach can be. Think about how liberating and healthy the second approach can be. My editor Jen sees it as "attitude is what can impact your overall response." Attitude or perspective, both terms work for me. Apply whichever one fits with you better, then reflect on it—Which approach do you take in a situation? And if different, what variables affect the perspective you chose? In other words, what door locking situations are you hanging on to?

QUESTIONS FOR YOU TO PLAY IN:

What approach to experiences do you want to continue with in your life?

_____

_____

_____

_____

_____

_____

_____

Reflect on your current (formed by experience) habits.

What experiences are harbouring?

_____

_____

_____

_____

_____

_____

_____

What can you let go of? Free yourself of?

_____
_____
_____
_____
_____
_____
_____
_____

What new habits can you make to support this? (i.e. my inner voice now says "Nancy, you know you locked the door. You are not checking again. DRIVE AWAY FROM THE HOUSE!")

_____
_____
_____
_____
_____
_____
_____
_____

What will you start today, to adjust this?

_____
_____
_____
_____
_____
_____
_____
_____

14

Brand ME

I'm smiling. I'm smiling sitting here thinking about Ally McBeal. (13) I'm sure I'm dating myself and fortunately my hunch says a number of you are smiling along with me. Truthfully, I don't quite remember the year the TV success show Ally McBeal began—yet the internet informs me the show ran from 1997 to 2002. Quick background for those who don't know the show: Ally McBeal was a young lawyer who got into law by following her then boyfriend to Harvard. Years later (when the show starts), she find herself working at a law firm with him and his wife. The important part to mention for us to move forward—Ally was constantly working through who the heck she was, what she both wanted and didn't want, predicaments and fantasies in both her work and play life and she also was a tad quirky (understatement). Although I don't know anyone who was quite like her, many of us connected to some of the stuff she was constantly working through (there was LOTS of it so we had a buffet of options to choose from!).

So . . . there are two episodes of Ally McBeal that I remember clearly. One held a phenomenal scene that I used for over a year in a diversity session I use to facilitate. The other episode, relevant to this topic—was an episode about having a theme song. Yes, a theme song. And for those of you, who did watch Ally McBeal, sing it with me: "I've been down, this road . . . I've been Searching my Soul Tonight".

I've dabbled in this theme song concept a couple times in the last ten years. "what's my theme song going to be today?", "What song will get me through this situation better?," or "This is my song of the summer!". Recently though—I've been considering taking it to the next level. What's MY theme song?

To date my theme song needs to represent:

- Energy
- A beat that I can't help but move to
- A chorus that I MUST sing when the song comes on, regardless of where I am, because I just can't contain myself
- From the very first beat of the intro, it's got me smiling.
- A message about living fully or in life moments

So that's all I've got so far. I have found songs that the instrumental component gives me this—but the words don't connect for me yet. It'll come. And I look forward to it. I'll ask you about your theme song thoughts in a couple more paragraphs. For now, I want to challenge to you continue your thoughts about *Brand ME*. I'm referring to what you represent & what that looks like.

We, all of us individuals, are exactly that. Individuals. Amazing though how quickly we get plunked into groups through judgements and other stuff. I think the individual stuff is really important. And I'm kind of tired of the 'plunking'. As an individual, I'm standing stronger for 'my stuff'. The stuff that's important to me, the stuff I value, my opinion if I feel it's not clear or not heard. I represent me. And my theme will represent me. Kind of like a brand. Yes—the brand is me—and I'll need a tag line too! Tag lines/ Mantras I'll explore with you in the next chapter. For now, we'll focus on Brand ME based on what I shared in this paragraph. To explore what a Brand is made up, I mind mapped it and found that the items that I came up with fall into four buckets which then all can be poured into Brand ME.

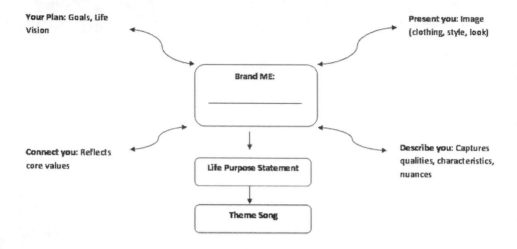

As you look at this diagram buckets or categories may need tweaking to suit your need. Please edit and add buckets so this exercise fits you.

With fourteen chapters of *The Happy Place* read and thoughts captured in note form at the end of each section, you've explored some of these areas for yourself already. I've listed some questions for you below on overall Brand ME, to assist you with your continued exploration and there is also a Brand ME diagram for you to record your own buckets. I suggest you first see what first comes to your mind and then refer to your chapter notes to find other items to include.

I started with theme song because that what's came up for me. My rule of thumb is 'go with the gut'. My gut said theme song, so that's where I started. Looking at the list I captured for you on what's important to me, in rereading it I easily linked my theme song *wants* to my values. Here's my list a second time, with values of mine listed beside them in italics.

To date my theme song needs to represent:

- *Energy*
- A beat that I can't help but move to *movement and action*
- A chorus that I MUST sing when the song comes on, regardless of where I am, because I just can't contain myself *captures full attention, pulls me to be fully present*

- From the very first beat of the intro, it's got me smiling. *Connection*
- A message about living fully or in life moments *positive, powerful, inner strength*

It's exploring time. I'm asking <u>you</u> to explore <u>you</u>. There is no right or wrong in this, simply awareness. See what comes up for you and keep it easy. Start with the diagram or the questions below and record any thoughts that come to the surface.

What's your theme song (list anything that comes to mind):

_____

_____

_____

_____

_____

_____

_____

Feel stuck—then email friends and ask them—"if you had to choose a theme song for me, what would it be?"

You're half-way through *The Happy Place* now. Reflect on the experience so far. What life themes are coming up for you specific to who you are (your presence, how you handle situations, your habits, your friendships, your work values)?

_____

_____

_____

_____

_____

_____

_____

_____

What themes or areas would you like to add to your life?

_____

_____

_____

_____

_____

_____

_____

_____

What is Brand YOU about?

_____

_____

_____

_____

_____

_____

_____

_____

How would a close friend, sibling or parent describe you?

_____

_____

_____

_____

_____

_____

_____

_____

What words would your boss, colleague or client use to describe you?

_____

_____

_____

_____

_____

_____

_____

_____

Using the Brand ME diagram, make notes under each category for yourself.

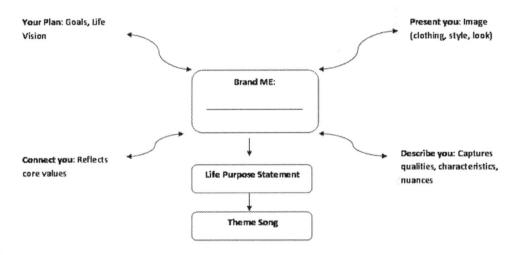

Go to http://lifedots.ca/connect-with-your-dots-template/ for larger printable worksheets.

With this awareness, please make some action steps for yourself. This may include things like getting assistance in connecting with and labelling your values, working with an image consultant to connect inner you with outer you, asking others for insights on what qualities they see in you.

I suggest you fold this page down in your book. As you continue reading, the chapters will prompt other items that will fit under one or more of the categories.

In my opinion, Brand ME is an ongoing process and a wonderful clarity-granting journey. You might not be closing this chapter with your brand being crystal clear, yet you are more aware than you were three pages ago.

Once you have enough captured under each bucket (your gut will tell you), considering all these findings, ask yourself, what word or words best captures this for me. Please push yourself to come up with a minimum of seven options.

_____

_____

_____

_____

_____

_____

_____

_____

Looking at your list above, circle three that resonate with you.

One circle at a time, try each on. Wear it for a week. Choose what fits. Maybe you just got a brand.

15

IF IT DOESN'T SCARE YOU . . .

Truthfully, I'm not sure exactly when I took this saying on yet sometime in 2010 I decide on a new mantra for myself which is 'If it doesn't scare me it's not worth doing'. I don't know if I read it and it resonated with me, or if I heard someone state it and I though "yaaaaah, I like that!" And, it doesn't matter where it came from. What matters is both what it's given me and where it's taking me.

As a public speaker (a.k.a. facilitator, key note speaker, presenter, group coach etc) there is a length of time prior to getting in front of your audience-to-be that my stomach does the 'flip'. You know that flip I am talking about. It can be a combination of any of these: 'yikes', 'am I going to be sick?', 'what if I don't present the material properly?', 'what if the audience is disengaged?', 'what if I screw up?', 'I'm about to stand in front of an ENTIRE group of people and be listened to', etc. Thoughts of doing a speech in front of your class in grade school or a recent presentation at work may have brought up a similar feeling for you.

A perspective I now focus on every time I feel this is: IT MATTERS. When my tummy is flip flopping like a fish on land, it's because whatever I'm about to do matters to me. Empowering. So I turn that flip-flop to strength. I acknowledge internally what specifically matters to me about the situation, the preparation I've done to be successful, and the self-critique I will do after to learn from the experience. And then I go deliver. If I don't have that flip, I know I'm in trouble. To me that means it's not important to me (anymore) which is vital in my business because if I'm not feeling connection and resonance to the content and the session, how can I possible expect that or hope for it for the participants?! Hear and feel how different this approach is then the first option ("YIKES!")

and imagine the impact it can have on a session. I know you've heard from me a number of times now how important emotional connection is for me. This flip flop phenomenon is like emotional investment. You need to decide when it comes "do I stay and invest (because it matters to me) or do I go (and lose out on the opportunity to experience and learn).

When I read Andre Agassi's autobiography <u>Open</u> (15) he speaks to his 'tummy experience' this way: *"Butterflies are funny. Some days they make you run to the toilet. Other days they make you horny. Other days they make you laugh and long for the fight. Deciding which type of butterflies you've got going (monarchs or moths) is the first order of business. Figuring out your butterflies, deciphering what they say about the status of your mind and body, is the first step to making them work for you."* This resonated with me. I like Andre's (and his coach Gill Reyes) approach to categorizing the stomach butterfly. My take from this passage is—Let's name or label it, find out more about it and put some characteristics to it. Then I will know what "I'm dealing with" and approach it best, and to my advantage. How's that for owning your energy?! I love it.

So—back to my mantra of "if it doesn't scare you it's not worth doing". How am I living this? Well, I'm repeating myself from another topic I know yet, it's worth the repeat: Your gut is always right. It's the interpretation of your gut that can screw things up. I am a STRONG believer of this.

When my tummy does this flip-flop/butterfly thing I connect with it. I ask myself 'What's going on here?!" then I sit back to feel/be with what my gut is truly saying. We have a gut for reason. It's like our own protector. How lucky are we! What's unfortunate is that many of us have been taught not to listen to our gut but instead to obey what we've been told to do. So the signals (flops) that our gut generates we interpret for a different meaning. No wonder it's so *flippin'* confusing! So I am now retraining my head on my guts cues. I am still learning what the various cues mean and how to respond to them accordingly.

Example from my past when I didn't listen to my gut:

- I had THE BEST hand-painted Wonder Woman snowboard. I was walking into the ski chalet for a quick washroom break and then heading straight back out to the hill. My gut was SCREAMING at me. My (wrong) interpretation allowed me to leave my board with the rest of the equipment by the chalet entrance door. I was back outside within 5 minutes and my board had been stolen. GONE. I loved this board. My gut, ME, knew from the feeling I had that I wasn't to leave it unlocked. I over-rode the internal messaging "flip" with pathetic 'logic'. Eight years later and I still remember the sensation that I ignored that day.

Some examples from my past that I did listen to my gut:

- Just out of University, I was volunteering at an athletic charity event, and on my volunteer break I joined a team of guys throwing the football around. Chatting with a bunch of them, one ends up being the VP of a sales and marketing agency. Leaving to go back to my volunteer duties he says to me, "I think you are a match to our organization—you should apply to work with us". I say thanks and scamper off to volunteer. Within 2 minutes of getting back to my volunteer post my tummy flip starts. And what I loved was its powerful scream "You GET OVER THERE and ask that man for his business card and get a resume to him immediately". Could I have skipped this? Yes. Continued to volunteer and forget about the conversation. Sure. But, I stood in the flip. Took it in. Grabbed energy from the flip and walked back over to the man. That was Saturday. The company was at the time called the Sales and Merchandising Group. My resume was to my football contact that Monday morning and my first interview that Friday. My career would not be where it is today, without them. Way to go, gut!
- Asking my then husband for a divorce. What was my logic saying? I could write two pages here including concerns of my extended family's reaction, having to tell our sons, changing everything we know, etc. What was my gut saying? *You need to do this. Today.* This feeling is from the unknown ahead, and living the life you're supposed to have. The initial calmness I felt after the conversation . . . I can't even attempt to put words to.
- Remember that company that asked me to go facilitate in Italy . . . and then it fell through? Couple weeks later they asked if I could

do another European adventure. I already had another work gig booked and I could have pulled some strings to move the date. My gut said: 'do not move your booked gig until the Europe gig is confirmed in writing'. I communicated quickly and rationally through the offer, stating options and needs prior to going ahead with the work. Four days later, the work trip to Turkey was reneged.

Ok—so what's this tell you? I'm starting to use and rely on my gut; my body's natural way of taking care of itself, and it working.

My coaching friend Stuart shared with me recently that often our life's biggest regrets are things we didn't do, not things we did do. I agree with this statement and see that it can easily be paralleled: *ignore gut = (potential) big regret*

Let's apply this back to my mantra "if it doesn't scare you, it's not worth doing!"

My gut is there to take care of me. And my life is here to live it just once. So I now use my gut at a whole different level to decide on the adventures I take on. If the flip is a "good flip" I'm in, if it's a "flop" I'm calling it then and there. So . . . some good flips in the last 4 months:

- Booking Greece flight. On my own. No travel partners. No hotel plans. Just making it happen.
- Writing this book.
- Approaching a family member with a touchy issue. Yes, I could have let it fester but by not letting it fester, the "ugh, it's going to be a tough conversation" was alleviated within 20 seconds
- Approached a potential client that I did an RFP (request for proposal) for, with a more suited candidate than me to do the work for him.
- Investing my savings differently then I have ever before. (Still saying yikes here, but doing it)
- Told a client that I could no longer work with them.

- On line dating (and for your interest it was short lived yet Wowser what a terrific experience for me and really help me define what I want in partner and . . . what I don't!)

So—my approach with my new mantra of *If it doesn't scare you, it's not worth doing* is coupled with me taking risks and being vulnerable.

What I am learning from this includes how much others are appreciating this, how much this approach is giving me and teaching me about myself and although the outcomes might not be 100% stellar, the journey provided the nuggets I need to move my life forward to my next (even better) thing.

Two mantra's ago (12ish years ago now) was 'Openness, Honestly, Vulnerability'. I strived for that, and now it's part of me. It was time for a new mantra level. And my gut tells me this one's going to be around for a while!

CHALLENGE FOR YOU:

What mantras have you admired of others?

_____

_____

_____

_____

_____

_____

_____

_____

What mantras (secretly or openly) have you had for yourself in the past?

_____
_____
_____
_____
_____
_____
_____
_____

Now 80+ pages into this book, what's your gut telling you about what you want to do for yourself/your life?

_____
_____
_____
_____
_____
_____
_____
_____

What mantras are you will to try on for yourself, starting today?

_____
_____
_____
_____
_____
_____
_____
_____

16

STICK YOUR CHEST OUT, ON THE INSIDE

My son was 5 years old when he started playing hockey. After one of his games I caught myself smiling (both on the outside & the inside) thinking about his third game of the season—he scored two goals. I am acutely aware though, that although I am proud of him & excited for him about the goals, I am more enamoured with his tenacity. Nate's on the ice as early as 7am for some games and practises. He had never held a stick before the season began and was just grasping "the walk skate". He had fallen how many times and without skipping a beat bounced back up and 'chased' both the puck & his team mates.

I am in awe of his curiosity and ability to learn the sport as quickly as he is. I am wowed by his attitude regardless of how many times he has fallen or missed the puck. And I am thrilled that he is learning the importance of what team means. That's where my pride comes from. That's why I am proud of him.

I think Nate feels his own pride for everything I just shared with you. I see it in the sparkle in his eye and hear it when he replays the experience for me. This got me to thinking about us adults . . . How often do you really, truly feel pride or proud of yourself? And what do you do to celebrate?

I was working with an International client last year. He had recently completed his Masters Degree holding marks in the top 10 percentile of his class. I asked him what he was doing to celebrate this accomplishment. He told me that he was looking for a job. I then repeated my question, *what are you doing to CELEBRATE what you did to achieve such an accomplishment?* The question sunk in the second time. It was a neat moment for both of us.

Something changes in us between Nate's sweet age of 5 and adulthood. Maybe it's assumed that we're supposed to be completing good things and that once one is accomplished, it's time to RUN and start the next one. In my opinion, that's a shame.

I want to challenge you on engaging yourself with yourself—both your strengths and your pride pieces. This will help you keep your Life Dots connected.

I do this 'exercise' for lack of a better word with my sons when we cuddle. I'll ask them one at a time, *Sweetheart what's great about you?* and we create a list. I think this is important for them to be clear on who they are and what their strengths are. Because if they can identify the traits in themselves, I believe it keeps the traits strong in them and others may benefit from it too. I think it's just as important to you. So, it's your turn *Sweet Reader. What's great about you?*

_____

_____

_____

_____

_____

_____

_____

_____

_____

_____

_____

_____

_____

_____

_____

_____

Challenge time. This list needs to hold a minimum of 25 items. Include characteristics, skills, capabilities, unique human trick that you are great at. What makes you YOU.

_____

_____

_____

_____

_____

_____

_____

_____

_____

_____

_____

_____

_____

_____

_____

_____

_____

_____

Now imagine a time in the last 10 years that you did something you were really thrilled about. You worked at something and accomplished the task, you pushed through your comfort zone and did something radically different from your usual or you gave in a way that made you feel great internally. Describe the situation AND how it made you feel.

_____

_____

_____

_____

_____

_____

_____

_____

_____

_____

_____

_____

_____

_____

_____

_____

Now here's where I want to play with you. That sense of pride. That *standing taller and prouder, smiling on the inside, I just WOW'd myself and connected with a value important to me* feeling. How would feeling like this more frequently impact your day? Nah, better question for you: How would feeling like this EVERY DAY positively impact your year?

_____

_____

_____

_____

_____

_____

_____

_____

_____

_____

_____

_____

_____

_____

_____

_____

I might seem like I'm 'talking crazy talk' suggesting you feel like that every day. And guess what—I'm okay with that. I want you to be clear on how acknowledging yourself can both keep you connected to you and your values, as well as impact all those around you.

Ensuring we are clear: I am not speaking of over-confident, all about 'yourself' arrogance. Far from it.

I am speaking about you being clear on you, your offering and thriving from it. I consider this healthy self-awareness. In my opinion there's a huge difference.

On the opposite side of the spectrum there's the lack of awareness, going through the motions, unconnected to the WOW of results that lots of people seem to miss in an average week. Ugh.

Individually, we all deserve this skill to do this for ourselves, and the time to enjoy what it gives us. Wonder if you're willing to give it to yourself and let all around you, including you, enjoy the impact.

If you want to do some more exploring:

What successes have you had in the last 10 years?

_____

_____

_____

_____

_____

_____

_____

_____

_____

_____

_____

_____

Looking at the above list, how many of these did you celebrate?

_____

If you answer was 90% or more, YAHOO and CONGRATULATIONS. Move to the next chapter and KEEP IT UP!

To the rest of you:

When did you stop celebrating you and why?

_____

_____

_____

_____

_____

_____

_____

_____

If you won't take the time to celebrate you, who will?

_____

Describe how you will make celebrating you a priority and why you need to do this.

_____

_____

_____

_____

_____

_____

_____

_____

I can't see what you've written down for yourself. I wish I could.

If you're happy with your findings for yourself in this chapter, terrific and please make a plan to celebrate one of the things on this list by the end of the month.

If you feel you're not deserving of celebration, take the time to uncover why. We all have a starting point and you deserve yours too. XO

17

You win some, you lose some

Recently I was reading an article about life. It was detailing people's outlooks and expectations about what day to day life is all about. It got me thinking about . . . well, a lot of things.

Recall any of these sayings?

- You win some, you lose some
- That's the way the cookie crumbles
- Too good to be true
- There are plenty of fish in the sea
- Every path has its puddle
- It's a blessing in disguise
- All is fair in love and war
- Good things happen to those that wait
- There's a light at the end of the tunnel
- When there's a will, there's a way

What do they give you?

Hope. Encouragement. Peace. Reinforcement. Relief. . . . . . other?!

Many of these sayings, (other than the puddle one) I've heard my whole life. My hunch is that you recognise a number of them too. My take is that since I was old enough to comprehend things, I heard these sayings to encourage me to look at the bright side of things, to motivate me to stick with the task at hand, to inspire me to get through a situation, to believe there is better coming in my future. They are lovely, help me to put or keep things in perspective sayings.

With common sayings like, 'you win some, you lose some,' when I have heard this saying in the past, I attach it to a specific situation. For example—you can win some and lose some soccer games. Or you can win some and lose some business pitches. What didn't register is that this applies to life overall.

What's hit me though is what opportunity we're skipping over here. **An opportunity to look at the big picture. The big picture of life.**

I just throw out there . . .

How many people expect that life should be good or even great? You go to school, get good grades, get your first job, work long hours, slowly build your career, and things (life) should all fall in line.

What if instead we saw life as a pool of experiences?

Some are quick dips.
Some are fancy dives off high platforms.
Some are leisurely swims.
Some are training laps.
Some are endurance races.
Some you can only dip your toe into.
Some you need a life jacket for.
Some you must use a raft.
Some you must use a paddle.
Some involve many people and a net.
Some involve rules, regulations and a referee.
Some require a partner.
Some require a team.
Some require buoys and markers.
Some are synchronized to music . . . .

My observation is that many people expect that life should be X. And X amount of this X equals good things.

I would like us to consider another approach—What if individuals' expectations of life were adjusted to suggest that 'your life journey will give you the pleasure of experiencing all that you can from the full spectrum of experiences'? From an emotional perspective this includes every adjective you can list; happy, sad, joy, grief, anger, resentment, hatred, love, fear, hardship, loss, thrill, etc.

Would this better manage a "good" day from a "bad"? Would this alleviate the word "good" from day and therefore allow all days to have their own measurement stick based on the experience and now the "wow factor".

After experiencing a 'glum' day last week, I got to thinking and then verbalized to a friend: "I'm okay with a glum day. I need to sort through the glum stuff to know what's in my inventory . . ."

In other words, I've adjusted my view on my days. Before, my approach was that a good day was a GOOD DAY! A bad day was "ERRR!" Instead of expectations of "good days" and "bad days" it's what I experience within each day (could be a combination of lots of good and yeesh things!) that doesn't label the full day good or bad. Kind of like on a diet.

Let's say we start a diet on Monday. We are doing "well" until Monday at 2pm and we eat 3 cookies. We label the day a bad day and then continue to eat cookies for our dinner main course . . . What's the good day/bad day label give us?! Nothing but trouble! You can end up mislabelling, mismanaged expectations and potentially creating a lack of connection with some good stuff and good learnings in your day. My learning is that to be with the emotion of the 'bad' within the day allowed me to open back up faster and get more great from the day versus ruining it with a full day label of bad. I've also learned to appreciate all that my emotional range allows me to experience.

For me to best 'squeeze the life sponge' of my day, is to start each day with an empty, dry sponge. Then when I experience an emotion from the pool of life, I can be fully present to it, versus rating it on a good/bad-o-meter.

So—good day, bad day, or a new day of experience? Which is your approach?

I think many of us assume that it should work out all the time. And when things go wrong its shock: "Well what happened and why didn't things go as planned!?" Of course, we want things to work out as much as possible yet, so much of the good times being great is taking the learning moments in the journey to make the finish product WOWIE!

Crap happens . . . . often.

It is how we handle it that makes us who we are.

And the next steps we take clearly show what we learned from the experience.

There's a lot to be said for the journey.

QUESTIONS FOR YOU TO CONSIDER:

When was the last time you labelled one of your days a good day or bad day and describe the day.

_____

_____

_____

_____

_____

_____

_____

_____

How did labelling that specific day impact the rest of your day?

_____

_____

_____

_____

_____

_____

_____

_____

When it's a labelled bad day, what currently do you do to learn from both the situation and the outcome?

_____

_____

_____

_____

_____

_____

_____

Taking a guess that the answer to the above has the potential to do more: What else could you do to learn from a situation or outcome in your day?

_____

_____

_____

_____

_____

_____

_____

What is tough for you not to have? (I.e. Control? Teamwork? Money? Respect? Trust?)

_____

_____

_____

_____

_____

_____

_____

Do any of the above listed things impact your day consistently?

_____

_____

_____

_____

_____

_____

_____

_____

What awareness has this exercise provided for you to take away to work on/apply/reflect?

_____

_____

_____

_____

_____

_____

_____

_____

18

IT'S QUITTING TIME!

When is it time to quit something? GREAT question! Yet foolishly many of us ask ourselves this way too late in the situation. Reflecting on the chapters we've shared so far, think about it . . . how many times have I asked you about your plan? For example, here are a few of the questions I've asked: What will you do to start this action today? Who will support you in being accountable to this plan? How will you make this happen for yourself now? In other words . . . . WHAT'S YOUR PLAN?! When you try something out, something new, do you agree with yourself or with someone else, how long you will try for before you will "play or pass", "quit" or "move on"?

In life we try things often, especially in our younger years, to see what we like and don't like, want to do more or less of, connect with our interests, and avoid our 'boredoms'. It's a process we go through, a process of elimination, a smart and sensible one. I remember being involved in a ton of activities when I was little: tap dancing, baton twirling (both skills very useful in my job today), swimming, diving, guitar lessons, skiing, skating, baseball, etc. The parental directed approach was, you try it for a session or season and then my parents would have the conversation with me on whether or not I liked it enough to do it again. Process of elimination—smart, simple, sensible.

So then what happen to us?

What makes us stick with things WAY longer than we should? You know what I'm talking about, yet to help you explore it deeper, I'll give you some examples:

- A friend of a friend, we will call her Patsy, was in a job she hated. She despised this job. She was unhappy, lacked energy, unmotivated, and truthfully, painful to be around because the negativity was like a dark cloud hanging over her. She asked to meet with me through our mutual friend to get some direction on how to move on. We shared a conversation (important for me to note: it was a dialogue, not coaching), which at the time seemed to go swimmingly well, and that was that. FOUR years later she finally resigned from the position. FOUR MORE YEARS. That's four years of her life in her 'unhappy place' . . . .

- A client I was coaching had been married for 15 years. She came to me for career coaching and then the coaching led to other things. She easily listed for me what she was missing from her spouse and relationship. She explained everything she had tried, everything he had attempted, the counselling, the special dates, the fighting, the inability to understand each other, etc. I asked, "What would need to change for this relationship to work for you at its minimum?" She listed 12 things. I then asked "If I gave you all the money in the world could you fix this situation?" she said no. "If I gave you the best relationship counsellors and support people would it fix this situation?" With hesitation she said no. I then asked, "What do you need to give yourself to move on from this situation?" She said, "Permission to quit".

We, us human beings, we 'less-than-perfect, trying-so-hard-in-this-life-of-ours' human beings can set ourselves up with some pretty high standards and expectations. In chapter six we dove into some insights on where and how these expectations are developed as we grow up. Some internal one-liners you may recognise include:

If we agreed to try it, we need to make it work.

If we bought the equipment for the sport, we need to use it.

If we signed up to participate, even though it's causing blisters, bone rubbing and stress, we need to see it through.

If we took the degree at school, we must work in the affiliated field or industry for the rest of our lives.

All the above statements are noble. They speak to pride, a sense of loyalty, and truth to our spoken word.

I'm not suggesting we go back on our word to others or ourselves. Ever.

I'm suggesting we reinvent our contract and think through what we sign up for, before we sign on the dotted line.

Let's look at some examples:

- Instead of committing to the sport of snowboarding by buying the equipment; rent the equipment for a full weekend, pay for lessons and thoroughly try the sport out. At the end of the weekend decide "play or pass."
- Starting a new job, your stomach is doing the 'flop' (versus the flip of encouragement we're looking for) give yourself a 30, 60 and 90 day plan to decide on your long-term commitment to the company and position. That's what the company does with you. Take this time to decide if this is truly the right fit for you, your skill set, your career aspiration. At the end of the 90 days have a 'stay or go' strategy in place.
- Relationships old and new, a reminder from the chapter called *Parameters* where we talked about designing an alliance. Know what your wants and needs are. Speak them clearly. Prioritize them for yourself in importance. Try it out. Give yourself a "try-out period". Then make a decision, in or out. Or, in existing relationships, reassess what your needs and priorities are. Do you have a friend that is consistently late and you are done waiting? Or a fair-weather friend? What do you need for the relationship to work for you? What would make you stay in the relationship versus quit or adjust it?

What makes us waiver on quitting? Some common excuses (with my responses in italics) are:

"I dunno, maybe it will get better . . ." *(Better than what? What you've just described sounds like rock bottom!)*

"I'll just give it another 6 months" *(Come on! If the last three years are any indication, this isn't going to change!)*

"Well, what other options do I have?" *(ARE YOU KIDDING ME?!?! The rest of your life happier is one of your many options.)*

What allows YOU to settle?

_____
_____
_____
_____
_____
_____
_____
_____

What excuse do you use most?

_____
_____
_____
_____
_____
_____
_____

List five more.

Come on—get them out of your system:

1. _____
_____

2. _____
_____

3. _____
_____

4. _____
_____

5. _____
_____

There are some distinctions to be had here.

Off the top of my head (sorry *Webster Dictionary*):

Settling—accepting something that is less than the standard you deserve

Quitting based on plan—the ability to access a situation, understand your threshold of skill and interest, and make a decision to stop because you are not getting what you want or need from it

Failure—lack of success. Loss, of a lot . . . credibility, self esteem, confidence, trust.

Notice the difference when you read those? YEESH to settling and failure. It makes me feel negative just reading them. Quitting based on plan is a different approach.

What I am suggesting is that when you try something, ANYTHING, you have an opportunity to approach it with a different spin. It's not about failing. It's about coming up with and agreeing to a 'trying it out' plan, learning from the situation, and knowing if or when to quit.

Imagine approaching new situations from this perspective and how different the experience, the learning and the residual would be for you:

1. When you try something new, have a plan in place (timeline, measurables, objectives) for when it's time to quit or forge ahead.
2. Set parameters that align with what you truly want and value in life. Consider what your response will be if things get misaligned for how you will handle it.
3. Be accountable for your own actions. You stay in something for the wrong reason, remind yourself who's at fault. Take a look in a mirror if you forget.
4. And a subtle push from me: "If it doesn't scare you, it's not worth doing"

QUESTIONS TO PLAY IN:

What came to your mind (about yourself/situation) while you read this section?

_____
_____
_____
_____
_____
_____
_____
_____

When was the last time you set yourself up for success when trying something new? (versus the thought/feeling of failure).

_____
_____
_____
_____
_____
_____
_____
_____

In your own words, how will you now define settling, quitting with a plan and failure?

_____

_____

_____

_____

_____

_____

_____

_____

What situations are you in today that you need to re-establish a plan for, to allow for a quitting plan, if necessary?

_____

_____

_____

_____

_____

_____

_____

What's your plan to action this?

Include objectives, expectations, specifics details, and timing.

_____

_____

_____

_____

_____

_____

_____

19

READ BETWEEN THE DOTS

My energetic sons are 16 months apart. For any of you reading this whom have birthed children, you know that's pretty close together. My "baby brain" second time around was like a large speed bump. I remember speaking to my neighbour Sue while standing on our lawn. I said "You know, the red thing the firemen use" while pointing at "it". She says ". . . fire hydrant?!" Yes, that was my delayed brain. So when I decided I wanted to start my own business after having the boys, I quickly realised I had some work ahead of me to literally get my head back in the game!

A past colleague shared with me his new-found love of non-fictional book reading versus newspaper and magazines. His motivation came from a friend of his who referred him to read a book called "Love is the Killer App" by Tim Sanders. (16) The past colleague of mine couriered the book to me the next day . . . and then I began. Tim's book taught me how to choose non-fictional books that would benefit me in both my career and my life, based on my interests and my required competency base for my role. His book them directed me through a process of how to read a book and *own* the content, enhancing my knowledge base and deepening my expertise in the skill/competency. This process includes everything from a note-taking system within the book, to how to bring the book up in conversation with others for both knowledge share and compassion. Five years ago April this book tip was passed to me, and I still hold strong to it today. Every month I read a non-fictional book, cover-to-cover, and then spread the wealth. On my website, www.lifedots.com I then write a blog debriefing my learning from the book which I fondly call "Reading between the Dots"

In one of *The Happy Place* first chapters you completed the Wheel of Life exercise. One of the spokes in the Life Wheel is Personal Growth. This is one of the things I do for myself for my Personal Growth life spoke. It allows me to continue to enhance my competencies specific to my career, based on the books I choose to review. It keeps me abreast of latest trends in both industry and in leadership training. It gives me natural conversation starters with friends, at networking engagements, at parties. I can apply my learnings & new insight to all aspects of my life. And the accountability to my website, webinars and blog readers makes me stick to completing the monthly readings.

Personal Growth can be experienced in a huge array of forms. Here are a few examples:

- Accreditation courses
- Reading
- Webinars
- Conferences
- Training courses
- Information sessions
- Mentor programs
- Volunteering
- Lectures
- Audio or DVD instructional recordings
- 8 week classes through community centers
- Correspondence courses
- DIY projects
- Journaling

Lots of people leave school & think "Great, I'm done with school—now to the real living!" For me I want to be learning until the day I die. In classroom environments I've done three rounds of post secondary education and four rounds of certification levelled accreditations. Outside the classroom my adult learning courses have included tap dancing, sky diving, self defence, cooking, quilting, tennis, meditation, volleyball skill training and counselling. I've participated in information sessions on real estate, financing and social media. I recently began utilizing my cardio workout time with audio non-fiction book 'listening'. Once a quarter, I participate in either a conference, webinar or key note speaker presentation. What I am aware of: Keeping it WOWie and stimulating my interests to want more. For me to be able to keep my Life Dots connected, the learning between the dots is important. In my opinion, it's Key.

So . . . The above *Personal Growth options to learn* list is just the beginning of how I'm going to consistently keep learning a part of my life. What about you? You've done some work while actively participating in this book, specific to your Life Dots. How about the stuff that connects your Life Dots together?

Name 10 things you would like to learn more about or improve your skills in:

1. _____

2. _____

3. _____

4. _____

5. _____

6. _____

7. _____

8. _____

9. _____

10. _____

Choose 3 from your list that you will make a plan to action starting by
_____ (date here):

1. _____
   _____

2. _____
   _____

3. _____
   _____

Outline the steps for each of the chosen three, to make this happen.

1. _____
   _____
   _____
   _____
   _____

2. _____
   _____
   _____
   _____
   _____

3. _____
   _____
   _____
   _____
   _____

What will get in your way to achieving this?

_____
_____
_____
_____
_____
_____
_____

And what's your plan for getting around the answer you listed for the last question? (Because, in my opinion without seeing what you wrote, there is a chance that you just listed an excuse. And you are worth more than an excuse.) Make it happen!

_____

_____

_____

_____

_____

_____

_____

_____

20

MMT

Using the chorus beat of the 1991 hit by Naughty by Nature called O.P.P. my inner voice is currently singing "I'm an MMT, ya you know me! I said MMT, ya you know me!" (17) Any guess what this acronym stands for . . . . MASTER Multi-Tasker. You know it's serious when there's an acronym!

So. Have I've got your attention yet? Was I singing your theme song a moment go?! My starting question to you—how did this happen to us!?!

Remember when you were four years old, playing with _____*insert your personal favourite child play toy or game here*___ and while playing we'd make lists in our head: "now after this I'm going to make a beaded necklace, then I'm going to go next door to play with Sam, come back to colour two pictures, do my letter practise, watch a show and then Mommy and I are reading stories.".

No! . . . . I don't remember this at all. Instead I remember idling blissfully in that joyful space called imagination. Simply playing with a content heart, fully absorb in the moment-by-moment experience of playing. How did we possible go from that to Master Multi-Taskers (MMT)?

What's scary is that I am fully aware of the list of 1001 reasons you are yelling at me, hopefully using your inner voice:

- I grew up!
- Those were the days

- Someone has to manage the *insert your biggest sore point* here: house/finances/family pressures/kids multitudes of activities/the extra work at the office, etc
- I'm exhausted
- All I do is chores
- House maintenance is never ending
- Laundry is fulltime job
- My paperwork struggle drives me CRAZY
- Because the bills need to be paid my dear!

Okay—so let's look at another perspective, what does the Master Multi-Tasker experience give you?

- A sense of accomplishment
- Keeps my household running smoothly
- Keeps me on top of *things*
- Retains my sanity . . .
- The thrill of a completed 'checked all' or crossed out to-do list.
- A (false) sense of control

Sure . . . . but, wait.

What does the MMT experience REALLY give you?

_____

_____

_____

_____

_____

_____

_____

_____

Stay here for a minute. Answer this question. Answer it for you.

One guess what the MMT experience gives me.

My confession: Nothing.

It gives me nothing.

Lots of short term stuff which I listed a minute ago but, long term it actually gives me regret.

When I had my first son, I'd run 14 errands in a day with him in the bucket car seat. I look at that now and think "foolish me". I could not tell you that any one of those errands were worth it. But I could tell you what I lost.

I lost the opportunity to rest and energise myself for the remainder of the day for both him and I.

I lost the opportunity to cuddle, coo, play and simply be with my baby.

I lost connection time. Just "BE-ing" time with him. I lost that for both of us.

Sure groceries need to be purchased, the family needs to eat for goodness sake. But look at all the things we put on our list above and beyond the "must do's" and then ask yourself, "what will this really give me?!"

I was a MMT through my wedding planning. Engagement Day to Wedding day was 16 weeks. And I pulled off insane things like crocheting baby blankets for all my bridesmaids, learning a choreographed dance for our first dance . . . Okay—now wait. I would actually repeat both those things. See—this is a good process to go through. It's the 'weed it out' process. I'll get back to the wedding day experience in a moment.

So as a Master Multi-Tasker—we have an AWESOME skill. We are extremely competent at getting things done. Let me say that again: YOU ARE EXTREMELY COMPETENT AT GETTING THINGS DONE. Others constantly say to you:

- You can get more done in a day than 5 people in a week!
- Listening to what you've done in a day is exhausting! How do you do it?!
- I don't know how you pull it all off.

This reinforcement . . . it's not helping. We hear it but, not really. Because our inner voice keeps saying "Be faster! Do more! Be faster! Do more!"

What I throw out there for all of us to ponder is—what is the MMTing worth to you?

As each of us knows, lessons in life need to be learned individually. There are things we wish we could do for others but they have to learn it for themselves. I gave you a bit of insight on my own experience/journey in what you've already read. Me writing specifically what I did to change the MMT in me won't actually make you get the process started for yourself. I'm sure you've realised from the questions I've been asking you in this book—the answers needs to come from you, for you to take ownership and accountability of your change. So let me spin it this way so I can still support the process for you.

Here's what I know:

The to-do list 'crossed it off' thrill only last for 15 minutes.

The MMT's Day is unachievable. The to-do list exceeds the capabilities of one person in a day. And you wake up every day with this new list. Every day you set yourself up with the responsibility of completing these to do's. Everyday. Everyday. Everyday.

We feel responsible for ourselves. For friends. For neighbours. For our community. For our children. For our extended family. So we make casseroles for the sick, volunteer at the school, church and hospital. We car pool, we knit booties for the preemies and coach soccer.

You're head nodding right now. Thinking "this is me, how does she know". Because there are a lot of us other there and I get it. It's exhausting yet, there is a bit of pride in it.

SO—MMTing has amazing, multi-level results to it. What can you do to hone in on your unbelievable ability while giving back to yourself?

If I was coaching you one-on-one, I'd take one approach with this. Since we're in book format, I'm going another route. Imagine the fun if we were coaching on this!!!

I'm going to dare you.

Ready for a challenge?

Interested in switching this up in your life?

From today forward, when you go to create your to-do list, use the following template.

Steps:

When you go to record a to-do, it must fall in one of the four quadrants. The lower the number, the higher the priority.

1	2
3	4

Once your list is made, you must complete the to-do's in your pre-ranked order. So we're clear: 1, then 2, then 3, then 4.

In each quadrant (1, 2, 3, 4) there are two listed areas "for me" and "for others". The 'for you' area tasks MUST BE completed before the "for others" in the quadrant.

The label for each of the quadrants draws from your application of chapter two. The *Must-Tick* quadrant is the priority quadrant because it's exactly what it stated. This MUST be done for me to TICK. The *Should Do's* you redefined for yourself in chapter two. Quadrant three captures things that if you didn't do them, you day would end at a similar spot yet when you get a couple nice to do's in, it meets your deeply rooted MMT need.

Quadrant 4 is only for your 'entertainment'. You can write as much as you like here. This is your "let it go column". Or your "if I do this it will cause more stress in my life because I am doing tasks that are unimportant to me instead of doing the GREAT THINGS I want to do".

Go to http://lifedots.ca/connect-with-your-dots-template/ for larger printable worksheets.

LIFE DOTS MMT LIST

Date:	
1. MUST-TICK	**2. SHOULD DO'S**
For Me: 1. 2.	For Me: 1. 2.
For Others: 1. 2. 3. 4. 5.	For Others: 1. 2. 3.
NICE TO DO'S	**SKIP**
For Me: 1.	For Me:
For Others: 1. 2. 3.	For Others:

Will you take on this challenge, from today forward?

Yes or No

What are you willing to lose by not doing this for yourself?

_____

_____

_____

_____

_____

_____

_____

Now—Let's hit pause for a second. Remember I told you I was going to come back to my wedding day example. Two things I listed for you that I took on in my sixteen week engagement-to-wedding experience were crocheting my bridal party baby blankets for the next chapter in their lives and taking dancing lessons to have the one and only 'Olympic-like performance experience' of my life. I would do both those things again (and again and again) because they are both SO who I am. I started both crocheting and dancing when I was really young and they meant a lot to me growing up and are now a piece of being. Giving to others and sharing what I like with those I care about are direct connectors to my values. Bingo! Satisfaction and talking about either of them now, ten years later still makes me feel good. Those were GOOD choices for me to complete and I happily worked my tail off to get that result. But what about all the other stuff I took on for the wedding!?! The help I denied because I could "do it myself (better)/do it my way/keep control/etc"? It exhausted me and took from others who cared about me and wanted to play a bigger role in this special day. Who lost? All involved. Who's to blame—me, the MMT.

My personal experience has taught me that the MMT thing wasn't actually giving me what I thought it was giving me; a sense of accomplishment, confirming that I was competent, even good at what I was doing and that this is what life was supposed to feel like day-to-day—"keeping up". The MMT lifestyle was actually taking away from the life I wanted. For me I thought when I got all the stuff done on the list, I could then have fun/ stop and smell roses, etc. Yet I would wake up the next morning with a new to-do list starting to percolate before my head had left the pillow!

Now I know that by trying to control so many to-do's, it was sucking the fun right out of me.

What did you think MMT/control was giving you? (Prior to 10 minutes ago)

_____
_____
_____
_____
_____
_____
_____
_____

And now reconsidering it (if that's changed) how do you see it now?

_____
_____
_____
_____
_____
_____
_____

I have GREAT news. You've spent years creating this level of multi tasking mastery. Now you get to apply it anyway you choose. See in life, we create habits, patterns for ourselves that we do again and again. Think for example about the ritual you follow in your daily morning shower or the route you take to and from work every day. I would hazard a guess that I could bet you a large sum of money that this "system", this "pattern" you follow is repeated daily. We're creatures of habit.

Name 5 MMT habits you MUST hold onto and what they give you.

_____

_____

_____

_____

_____

_____

_____

_____

What 3 new habits are you open to introducing to your life to give you more of what you want to do and less of what you 'to do'?

_____

_____

_____

_____

_____

_____

_____

_____

Will you commit to ripping up your to-do list at the end of each day and starting your next day fresh? This includes taking the ripped pieces to the garage garbage/ recycling, removing them from your reach, even burning them if you must.

Yes or No

Circle one.

Whom will be your go-to person for this life change you are about to make for yourself? You need to brief them on what change you are looking to make, as well as confirm with them that they are willing to play a role to support you. Define that role with them—what do you need from them? I.e. I will send you a one-line email saying "I am committed to doing less tasks and more for me. Today I enjoyed _____. My to-do list for the day is now in the garbage."

Draft what you need to say to that person.

_____

_____

_____

_____

_____

_____

_____

_____

Will you contact them RIGHT NOW and design the alliance you need for this to be successful for you?

Yes

(Only option! TAKE BACK YOUR LIFE.)

What's the penalty if you don't do this for yourself?

_____

_____

_____

_____

_____

_____

_____

_____

And just how will you celebrate when you do this for yourself? (Hint: celebrate each new phase, not just your final yahoo! You deserve it!)

_____

_____

_____

_____

_____

_____

_____

_____

21

HOW BIG IS YOUR NET?

Three birthdays' ago, I invited nine girlfriends over for dinner. My birthday is mere days away from Christmas and with the hustle bustle of the season, I've had many years of a blended "birthday and Christmas" celebration versus a straight on, Happy Birthday. To the point I tell people I celebrate Birthmas. My need to for focus on me for my birthday is low so I wasn't looking for a 'birthday party' yet instead to surround myself with some people I love and who love me, and to celebrate friendship and life. It was a wonderful evening shared with Thai food, wine and peanut butter and chocolate ice cream. I'd love to replicate the experience nightly!

A couple of days later, one of my friends at the dinner acknowledged her observation of the evening. She said "Nance, you've really got a BIG group of friends. I consider you one of my closest friends and yet I have only met two of the people who were at your table. It was eye-opening to me how many you had at the dinner as well as how much and how easily you were sharing about your life."

Gosh, I LOVE real friendship—what an interesting observation! It left with me something to consider and play with. My original take on it:

- Ironically, it was tough to choose nine friends to have to dinner. I had a large list, yet knew I wanted to be able to be seated at my dining table so nine it was. For years now, I have had lots of 'pockets' of friends—wonderful people that I've met from different areas of my life.
- I've been "really open" for a long time now (like 20 years)—not a surprise to you I'm sure, considering what I've shared in this book. I'm a big proponent of sharing life experiences and learning from

136

each other. Also, for me, connection if very important. Divulging "real" stuff, what makes you tick, and being vulnerable takes that connection and trust deeper. I love that!

With some reflection, I started considering how I balance friendships in my life. Remember the Wheel of Life exercise? When I did that exercise the first time it clearly identified where (in my opinion) I was misaligned with what I wanted in my life. It also left me thinking about what life spokes I may be overcompensating in to balance/counterbalance this misalignment.

From an openness perspective, HA—this isn't changing any time soon—it's something I like about me and others acknowledge what it gives them. What I've been left to consider though, is the potential of a 'levelling" program, sharing more with those friends at a "higher level" of relation.

My friendships make me tick. Authenticity, honour, trust, respect, fun, love, consistency, a comfort within self... I could go on and on. Friendship is amazing! Yet, Julie's observation was such an accurate one. By no means did she suggest I go "weed" my friend group, yet it did provide me another approach to my view on my friendships. How many *close* friends can one have and sustain at the quality-level that makes me tick?

Some background—I've always admired people who have two or three other couples they travel with yearly, with their families for a week. Or the five girls whom have been attached to the hip since grade 10. My perception is that they have a deep bond shared, sacred, like a sisterhood.

I'm also aware of lots of other perspectives that could go with that:

- They are friends through history, not through current interests
- They are friends through ease, not through connection
- They aren't spreading their wings, and are sticking to what they know

Either way—I've always thought the 'close knit' thing was neat. I've got a girlfriend that I've known since I was 8, another since age 11 and a third since age 13. I recently realized that only one of the three is a 'history friend' (definition—someone in your life because they are part of your history yet, little potential of a primary role in your future). So—I've got some extremely long-term relationships and lots more that are 10-15 years long. Yet, it made me think . . . how big am I casting my friend net?!

It is wonderful to have great people in my life. Yet am I spreading myself too thin and therefore not enabling the depths of friendships that I so desire? I already enjoy the level I have with my close friends—seriously, could there be more?!

I don't have an answer to this question yet. And yes, it's subjective anyway. Yet I'm going to explore it and see what I find.

We get caught in doing stuff that might not be the best thing for us. Are there things in your life that you may be doing for any of these reasons:

- Quantity versus quality (three Christmas parties in one night and not enjoying any of them fully, versus one great one)
- Things half-baked (too spent from doing other activities that when you finally get to what you want to do you're too exhausted to do/be your all)
- Spreading yourself to thin (a.k.a. guilt)
- The 'yes' person (a.k.a. guilt, wanting to please others and pressure to participate)
- Obligation (a.k.a. I should go, it would please my _____)

When I started writing about this topic, my thought was about 'the friend net', yet as I write I've thought about the various perspectives we could look at and really, the net can refer to any topic. For example *How big is your _____ net?* could be:

- Friend
- Chore
- Responsibilities
- Roles in life
- Debt to others
- Fallen behind with
- Ongoing projects to complete

- _____ insert name here _____

See what I mean . . . ! So when looking at the questions that follow, please don't settle with my example specific to spreading myself thin in friendships. Instead, sift through life areas of your own.

One other net idea I cast to you: How big is your net for "valued things for self"? Is it of equal size to your other life nets? Larger? Smaller? Continuing with the fish catching analogy; If your own net isn't your biggest net, where do you pull the strength and energy from to manage the other nets properly?

QUESTIONS FOR YOU TO CONSIDER:

What life nets do you currently have? List them all.

_____

_____

_____

_____

_____

_____

_____

_____

Reflect on them,

Which ones are working for you and what are they giving you?

_____

_____

_____

_____

_____

_____

_____

_____

Which ones aren't working for you and what are they impacting? (Either too wide, too small, too deep, etc.)?

_____
_____
_____
_____
_____
_____
_____
_____

What options do you have to adjust any of these nets? (Brainstorm ALL ideas here)

_____
_____
_____
_____
_____
_____
_____
_____
_____
_____
_____
_____
_____
_____

What three will you start today, to make this better for you?

_____

_____

_____

_____

_____

_____

_____

_____

Lastly, how about your net? (Ha—there was no chance I was letting that net go, in case you were hoping I forgot.). What do you need to add or edit within the catch of your own net?

_____

_____

_____

_____

_____

_____

_____

_____

_____

_____

_____

_____

_____

22

FUN-O-Meter

There were worksheets that both my boys were sent home from kindergarten with to help them recognise letters. Every page started with *Big _, little _ what begins with _?* So for example *Big H, little H, what begins with H? Happy Harriett humming, all begins with H.* We, the boys and I would come up with the examples of what began with the letter the worksheet asked for. I think this sentence structure is fitting for our next topic, FUN.

Big FUN, little fun, what begins with FUN?

Let's start with a definition of FUN. The Free Dictionary.com suggests this definition for us (18):

n.
1.   A source of enjoyment, amusement, or pleasure.
2.   Enjoyment; amusement: *have fun at the beach.*
3.   Playful, often noisy, activity.
intr.v. **funned**, **fun·ning**, **funs** *Informal*
To behave playfully; joke.
adj. Informal
Enjoyable; amusing: *"You're a real fun guy"* *(Margaret Truman).*
Idiom:
for/in fun
As a joke; playfully.

My guess is that you easily head-nodded in agreement to the definition provided for fun. Yet on a scale of 1 to 10, one being absolutely dismal and

10 being firecrackers off the roof of your home, how much FUN are you having currently in your life?

Record your number here: _____

If you scored 9 or more, WaHOOO! You are welcome to move to the next chapter or keep reading with the rest of us, for the fun of it. *Insert circus clown winky face here.* If you scored under 9, please stick with me.

First—the feedback I received from a *test* reader was *this isn't compelling enough for me to 'work' on it. How is this going to impact me?* This made me step back to consider how much laughter and fun people have in an average day. I wonder how many adults experience little to know fun in the day meaning this is now the norm and they haven't realised it's been missing. Because of where you are in the reading of this book, I'm going to assume that you're like me and not wanting a fun-less/ low level of fun life. Sharing another perspective on FUN in life, imagine kids playing. Picture the movement, feel the energy, hear the laughter. How often do we see kids in action and think 'remember the days when we stress free' or 'wish I could bottle some of that up." My perspective is that we all have this inside of us and somehow moving into adulthood it is SUCKED out of us. I'm not suggesting you install monkey bars in your office. I am suggesting that you consider and GET FREE with trying on fun in aspects of your life you either let it go or never had it. I had three corporate prospect meetings today. Three in a row. What a day. I could have raced around stressed about each meeting and the potential outcome. Instead I drove *and sang* between the meetings. Imagine what energy I was able to take into the after *sing-song car drive recess* meeting because of it. Who would you prefer to meet with: a) Happy, Fun girl who get your company results through Intentional Communication

Or b) Stressed, I hope this goes ok girl who gets your company results through Intentional Communication.

If you chose B, you're reading the wrong book (yet I'm intrigued on what's kept you reading!).

To get started on FUN integration, we need to first do some clearing.

In the last 10 years, detail 5 terrific fun experiences you have had, big or little.

_____
_____
_____
_____
_____
_____
_____
_____
_____
_____
_____
_____
_____
_____
_____

So, you've had some fun. Good. It's a start.

What's stopping you from having more/ daily fun in your life?

_____
_____
_____
_____
_____
_____
_____
_____
_____
_____
_____
_____
_____
_____

In my opinion there is only one thing stopping you from having more fun in your life. You.

Take a look at your list above. Reviewing the reasons you stated, what role do you play in any item on that list? After you have thoroughly gone through the list, I then ask you to consider what perspective tweaks (or monumental changes perhaps) are options for you to make in your day or life, to change this.

Let me give you a glimpse of some of the ones I have created to have more fun time in my life. We will define *fun time* in a moment.

- The nights I have my boys, school ends at 3:30 pm. My house rule is that I can only look at my email (insert your technology 'I'm too busy working' equipment list here) once I have tucked my boys in around 8:30pm. In other words, I unplug which in turn seems to allow me to plug in to me and my 'inner fun'.
- I asked my boys what having more fun with me would look like or be. They provided me a great list. I make the list a priority.
- I asked myself what having more fun would look like for me. I created a great list. I make the list a priority.
- I balance my calendar differently. I have revised my when to say yes & when to decline an invitation or request parameters.
- I now get daily *Must-Ticks* in my life. *See Chapter Two—The Word Should, if you require a quick refresher.*
- I'm living each year as my last. For example, this being my 40th year of life, it's my last time to experience to 40. So if I want to experience something in my 40th year of life, I make it happen. I'll share with you a snap shot of some of these things:
  o wanting more snow play time with family & friends so I've rented a chalet for the winter
  o taking a volleyball skills class so I sourced one for the one night a week my children are with their Dad,
  o and seeing Pink in concert in NYC at Madison Square Gardens because she's FUN.

Your turn: What adjustments can you make to how you are currently operating your everyday functioning, to allow space for fun, both big and little?

_____

_____

_____

_____

_____

_____

_____

_____

_____

_____

_____

_____

_____

_____

_____

Awareness of what you are both doing & not doing is fundamental for progress. Next let's define what kind of fun you are missing in your life. Please note that what I am capturing within each of the following buckets represents my subjective opinion of fun. Revise the list to suit you and your need.

BIG FUN:

- Vacations (to both new places or favourite places)
- Taking on something you have never done before (sky diving, mud racing, white water rafting)
- Fulfilling a dream (__insert dream here___)
- Something that would WOW you (being on a game show, riding a bull, touching the Stanley cup)
- Creating an adventure (bike tour of a city you've never been, training for and then climbing a mountain)

Little FUN: (my definition of little fun is something that I can do spur of moment versus monstrous planning)

- Cooking while dancing to great music
- Eating ice cream in bed for breakfast for my birthday (aka Birthmas)
- Firework hopping. *The boys and I literally, in pajamas, drive the neighbourhood scouting out firework displays. We jump out, we enjoy, we thank the provider & give a financial donation, and then drive to the next display we spot.*
- Street dancing. *When a favourite song comes on when we're driving, I stop the car on the side of the road and we dance.*
- Nurse head. *When the boys or close friends are sick, I have this blow up nurse's head I put on and then go visit them with balloons or homemade muffins. Always banana chocolate chip.*
- Once every 8 weeks I buy cards and send special notes to my friends and family to share with them what makes them extra WOWIE to me.
- Games. *We play them all the time. We make them up or go the traditional route. We play with each other and laugh and share as we go.*
- I welcome the unconventional. *Eating breakfast for dinner and dinner for breakfast, going commando because I can, skinny dipping, starting conversations with strangers, skipping when I feel like skipping, playing with the kids at recess and at the park versus parking my bones on a bench.*
- Laughing at myself. *This came a little later in life for me. I'm glad I've got it now. It's a wonderful gift and a freedom that in my opinion everyone deserves.*
- Revolving Doors. *I never miss the opportunity.*
- Jokes. *I have two child friend and two adult company only jokes always ready.*
- Gut laughing. *In my opinion, it's the only way*

Circle which you need more of in your life:

BIG Fun   Little FUN   Both BIG and Little Fun

Create your list. What would be fun for you (shape this list based on what you circled above).

_____
_____
_____
_____
_____
_____
_____
_____
_____
_____
_____
_____
_____
_____
_____
_____
_____
_____
_____
_____
_____
_____
_____
_____
_____

Circle a whole bunch of them that you really like. Get some stick-it notes and write one fun item on each note. Stick them everywhere—your walls, your mirrors, in your car. Read them and do them. Add them to your day.

Bring fun to your life as a noun, a verb and an adjective. Make fun a house rule and measure fun as part of your life goals or Wheel Actions.

I thought I was having fun before. Then, when I decided to get dirty with fun, like *plunge in the mud wrestle with fun*, I realised I had sometimes stood on the sidelines of fun, versus deep diving with it. Use you FUN-O-Meter and track where you are with fun today. And tomorrow. And every day. You get one chance to make this awesome life of yours WOWIE, and fun is definitely a part of that.

23

A Home is . . .

Regardless of your age, at one point in your life you've had a home. Through the years I've always interchanged the words house and home, thinking they are both the same thing. About 6 years ago I've realised that I define them quite differently.

The home I lived in four homes ago, I had built with my husband. Although a mass production home, we were so involved in the choices and process we really felt that we helped create it. Then, because it was a sub-division home, the neighbourhood all moved in within 12 months of each other, creating an unbelievable University frosh week zeal of 'WOW'! We were all experiencing similar things—decorating and buying furniture, watering our new sod and starting to landscape, trying out the schools, and working with the home builders to fix stuff. I think most importantly, we were all laying roots at the same time, to connect ourselves and our families to our new home and neighbourhood. My four years on Canyon Street is an experience I will always cherish. I think this community bonded because we, 'the people in the neighbourhood' were all going through such a similar experience at the same time, and we were all new to the sub-division. We started on a similar playing field. We started at a closer 'common ground'. And because of this, I think it opened us to meet more people and make more connections. As people, we often bond through commonalities. BINGO for this experience! This experience created a neighbourhood that felt like home, and it was REALLY tough on the heart strings to move for that exact reason.

My next home experience was a beautiful custom built house. But that's all it was for me. A house. The lack of connection with this second house was unreal to me. Regardless of the house's luxurious qualities, it could not compensate for what it lacked from the people living in it . . . love.

And then there is where I live now. I live in a town home half the size of my last place. When the boys and I moved in, everything we owned was stacked in my garage, other than a mattress for my basement floor, 3 pieces of luggage and my kitchen stuff. "Let the renovations begin!" and we lived like that—three of us sleeping on a mattress on the basement floor, for 6 weeks. And yet, this town home, in the first 48 hours, felt more like home than the custom built house ever did. So, in my personal reflection I started to play with, "What makes a home?". And what I realised is that a house, regardless of size, is a roof and four walls. A home is the stuff inside it. And let me make sure this is clear—when I say 'stuff' I don't mean purchased stuff. I mean the stuff that you love. I mean 'the stuff' that makes you miss home when you're not there. I mean the stuff that makes you smile on the inside because it gives back to you in the way you need to be given to. This list of 'stuff' is based on the needs of the individuals who are living there.

For me, my home is based on:

- Connection. Connection is a really important value for me in all aspects of my life. Specific to my home, connection is represented by things like warmth, comfort and emotional attachment. For me it's things like the pictures of my family displayed everywhere, sand and seashells from past beach trips sitting openly for me to touch, hues of blues and browns—colours that are earth/shore-like to me and keep me grounded and peaceful. It's using the fireplace as often as possible (heat is BIG for me).
- Ease. Every piece of furniture needs to be welcoming versus starchy. And although it's challenging for me to be completely 'at one' with the durability test my boys are conducting with the living room couch cushions through their fort making, they are living fully in their environment. And my inner voice again states "NANCY—it's a just a couch! Let them love our home for what it gives them!"
- Filled. I've lived in big houses in the past and sometimes felt lost in the cavernous space. For me every square inch of a home is meant

to be lived in. We've got enough space for individual time (also very key in a home for me) and enough space to live together. I think this has something to do with not wasting (a value for me) and respecting and enjoying what we do have.

- Feels good. I don't know how else to describe it yet I know what it feels like when I have it and when I don't. Ever walk into a room and think "yeesh, feel that tension" and then walk into another room and say "ahhhh, that's more like it"? Whatever your 'feel good' creation is, that's important to me in a home. When I'm home, I need to feel home. Cocooned, safe, connected. I've heard people talk about what comfort food or a comfort meal can give them—similarly, this is what I'm looking for from my home. It's like that saying 'It's nice to be home'.

Reflecting on my list above I am very aware of the first word I stated. Connection. Connection is one of my strongest life values. My home gives me connection through my creation of the space, the parameters it holds for the three of us and our guests, what and how I've decorated, and the safe space it gives my family to grow in.

Wow . . . this place of mine means more to me than I realised!

Hmmm . . . actually, let me rephrase that. My home and the space is creates for me and my boys, for friends, for family—it's a way that I give me to others, stay connected to what's important to myself and where I reenergise after being away. It's a safe space. It's home . . .

When we did the Wheel of Life exercise earlier, physical environment was acknowledged as one of the important pieces of your life. Physical environment speaks to your home, and for those of you who spend a lot of time in your car, car might fall in this category too. I had a client I was working with who rated her physical environment a three out of ten. When she detailed her answer she explained that although she liked the neighbourhood she lived in and their property they owned, she never liked the house. When she and her husband bought the place they had agreed to renovate as soon as they took possession. Seven years later, no work had been done, no plans were in place for renovations, no budget had been allocated, and no contractors had been met with. Imagine what it felt like for this person to live in this environment! How is one supposed to start their day with "POW!" when their home is sucking the energy out of them? Yikes!

Amazing the impact physical environment can have on you. And for sure, it impacts some of us more than others depending on the need for home connection or qualities from the environment that fill you. This makes me think of after being away at University, moving back in with your parents to save money for your first official place or to pay off school debt. Maybe not the best situation for all involved but a good short term solution to save money to get where you want to go. The impact depends on what the goal and needs are.

So back to you and your physical environment needs. Here are some questions to play in:

Think back to your childhood home(s). What fond feelings and memories come up for you?

_____
_____
_____
_____
_____
_____
_____
_____

And your current home—what do you like about it?

_____
_____
_____
_____
_____
_____
_____

Again for your current home—what would you change?

_____

_____

_____

_____

_____

_____

_____

_____

What would you have in your physical environment if there were no obstacles to get it?

_____

_____

_____

_____

_____

_____

_____

_____

Looking at some of your collected thoughts above, what do you need in and from your physical environment?

_____

_____

_____

_____

_____

_____

_____

_____

_____

_____

_____

_____

_____

_____

_____

_____

_____

How are you penalizing yourself by not having this/these?

_____

_____

_____

_____

_____

_____

_____

And what will you commit to today, to make this happen?

Short Term	Timing	Long Term	Timing

Go to http://lifedots.ca/connect-with-your-dots-template/ for larger printable worksheets.

24

YOUR HAPPY PLACE

An envisioned calm place.

What comes to mind when you read the term *The Happy Place*? For most, my guess is that it seems farfetched. Think about all the stuff that gets in the way of you and your happy place; job stress, managing a home, financial burdens, relationship challenges, etc.

Hmmm . . . that list isn't going to get us far is it. Bit of a mood spoiler. Let's go another route.

Three options:

1) *Complete this exercise by reading each line, then putting your book down & completing the instruction*
2) *Slowly read the lines below out loud while recording yourself. Then play it for yourself so you can go through the exercise without having this book in your hand, allowing you to focus on the exercise versus the instructions.*
3) *Go to www.lifedots.ca/videos. Search for The Happy Place visualization exercise. Find a comfy place to complete the exercise. Press play and follow my instructions*

Find a comfortable spot to sit or lie down in the room you're currently in.

Relax and just 'be' for a couple moments.

Agree to five minutes. Take longer if you need it. Clear your mind of the *other* stuff.

Connect with your body. Wiggle your fingers and toes, stretch your legs, roll your shoulders.

Breathe.

Enjoy it :0)

Once you are comfortably in the BE-ing place, focused on your slowed breath, thoughts turned to low.

Think about a time in your life that you were really happy. Immerse yourself in the memory as if you are living it for the first time.

When you can visualise it well enough that you can feel moment, stay in it. *Some areas to explore: What's around you (take it all in). What colours do you see? What's the temperature? What smells linger? What emotions are you feeling? What colours do you see?*

Take time here. Really take in the happy moment in your life.

When you are ready, capture it below.

What's the first thing that comes to your mind with your visual?

_____
_____
_____
_____
_____
_____
_____
_____

Describe it. Include colours, sights, details.

_____
_____
_____
_____
_____
_____
_____

What does is feel like? Share textures, smells, sounds.

_____
_____
_____
_____
_____
_____
_____

How does it make you feel when you are there?

_____
_____
_____
_____
_____
_____
_____

What does this place give you? (i.e. calm, slower heart rate, balance, etc)

_____

_____

_____

_____

_____

_____

_____

_____

What will you now call this place, to bring you back to this spot easily?

_____

_____

_____

_____

Sit here for a minute. Stay in this place. Feel it, breathe it, and connect with it. Keep it as real as possible.

The process we just went through; my questions, your thoughts, feelings, connections. This is now yours.

Stuff happens in our busy lives every day. Late for meetings, cereal milk spilt on my dress pants, bad traffic, delayed flights, screaming children. It all happens, daily.

We have options of how we want to manoeuvre through this day to day stuff. We can do it "our regular way" or from our happy place perspective. Yes, perspective; its key and its refresher time.

Let me give you a couple examples of how you can utilise the visual *Happy Place* you just connected with.

1) This summer I was working with a corporate coaching client via phone. This client is a ball of energy; go go go, high stress job, family dynamic challenges, devotes time as a volunteer on a couple boards

and is in a long distance relationship. Consistently when I speak to him he's upbeat, focused, driven. That day, he was just 'off his usual way. I, being me, called him on it. I've written it out in script below so you can follow clearly:

Nancy: "Frank, what's going on today, I'm sensing something is up?"

Frank then proceeds "Nancy, I tell you, I've just got a ton on my plate right now. The work is piling up on my desk by the minute, I've got 4 reports due by Friday, two employees resigned this week and I'm in court all day tomorrow."

Nancy: "Will you trust me and let me ask you a couple coaching questions?"

Frank: "Why sure, I've got nothing to lose!"

Nancy: "Okay—first, you've got 60 seconds to vent and clear everything that's going on for you right now. Ready—GO!"

Frank laughs and hesitates, I say "55 seconds", and then he starts listing at rapid speed!

Nancy: "5 seconds, and STOP. Okay, now Frank, tell me about a time when you were really happy."

Frank: "What?"

Nancy: "Will you try this for YOU? Tell me about a time when you were really happy."

Frank: A considerate pause. "Two weeks ago Saturday, while hiking with Stacey in the Blue Mountains"

Nancy: "Tell me about it"

Frank: "It was a beautiful day. The sun was shining—not a cloud in the sky."

Nancy: "What was the temperature like?"

Frank: "Perfect. Warm but not sticky"

Nancy: "Was there a breeze?"

Frank: "Slight, yet just enough"

Nancy: "What sounds were you hearing?"

Frank: "We were by a brook or something so the water gushing over the rocks, the birds chirping, our footsteps crunching our way through nature."

Nancy: "Any smells come to mind?"

Frank: "Fresh if that makes any sense. Maybe the breeze ignites that but it was like a 'fresh scent', earthy."

Nancy: "Frank, what will you call this memory for yourself?"

Frank: "A perfect day."

Nancy: "What do you feel like right now?"

Frank: Calm, relaxed. More grounded."

Pause

Frank: "Like me."

Nancy: "And taking this feeling. This calm, relaxed, grounded connection with you, to the work you need to get through this week, how will this approach change things?"

Frank: "Whoa. It's no big deal, I'll get it done. Stay focused on the right stuff, it will all happen. Nancy, how did you do that?!?"

Nancy: 'Frank, firstly thank you for trusting me. All I did was ask you some questions. You already have this perspective in your portfolio of 'great life stuff'. Simply, with all the work priorities piling up on you, you were moving into a crazier, "I'm losing control" perspective which we both know won't get you anywhere fast. You allowed yourself to connect to a great perspective, the perfect day that will allow you to function from a better spot, to get through this stuff you need to. What will you do if you lose grasp of this perspective?"

Frank: "Literally, stand up, breathe and imagine the sound of the water on the rocks and the sun on my skin. Wow, thanks Nancy. I really needed that."

Nancy: "Thank you Frank."

Although I shortened the script slightly and detailed a closing statement for you to assist the reader with understanding of the process completed, this was the conversation with client Frank. As the coach what surprised me the most was how WOWed he was by the outcome. For me, it was so within his grasp because of the energetic, connected perspective he usually functions out of, I learned from witnessing his experience of the coaching. As Frank described his *Happy Place* to me, line by line I could hear him entering it and getting deeper in it. His tone changed, his speaking pace, his breathing pattern.

So that's Frank's happy spot. Within that month, I heard from him. Both times to acknowledge that he's been consistently visiting this *Happy Place* of his and that it really works for him.

2) On the shore is my *Happy Place*. I told you a bit about it during the introduction and in the "Embracing the AHHH!" section. The shore for me is an endless beach of granular sand and soft waves. In my visual there are few people on the beach. The breeze catches my hair and keeps it at bay from my eyes. I'm sitting with my bum and feet in the sand, flowy, light linen-like cotton white button down shirt on, sleeve rolled to the elbow and a bather underneath. I sit. Sit and breathe. I hear the odd seagull but my real attention is on the sound

of the surf and the breeze. Relaxed, calm, at peace, connected, fully present, alive, alert to my senses, smiling from the inside out; happy.

I could write an entire page on my 'on the shore' *Happy Place*. And I share that with you because

1) Why would I possible hold back on sharing with you now LOL!
2) In my opinion, it's THAT important to be connected with the places you live best from.

When do I go to The Happy Place? At the beginning, I trained myself how to go there. Now, it's where I am every day, for as many minutes/hours that I can maintain it.

See, before I was functioning through my life. The MMT (Master Multi Tasker) in me was focused on doing tasks and things, all day long. I was doing a great job at it but, missing the life stuff I was hungry for. So, after my *The Happy Place* visualization experience, I started incorporating the *Happy Place* into my day. To the point now, I for the most part live from my *Happy Place* perspective and slip out only when something really dislodges me. I'm now three years into my official connection to my On the Shore *Happy Place* and was on a beach vacation last month. I had a tremendous week away yet, it felt different than it typically did. Then on a beach walk I realised what had happened. I have brought myself so into the *Happy Place* zone daily, and stick it, that my actual On the Shore *Happy Place* experience was already with me before my feet were on the sandy beach. My guess is that my last statement sounds crazy. I'm telling you truth and it shocked me as well. Insert the 'stick out your chest from the inside' pride moment here. Ta-Da!

Here are some examples of my personal examples of what impact this approach can have:

1. When the boys are behind with getting ready for school in the morning (DAILY). I have the option to:
   a) Yell (it gets none of us anywhere. I've tried it. No results and feel lousy)

b) Send them to school in their PJs and mints in their mouth because we've missed teeth brushing. (Disappointing but the mint is a negative reinforcement on skipping teeth brushing and wearing PJs to school for young kids is a thrill, not a consequence for behaviour)

c) Lose it (worse than "option a" and can impact everyone's day, for the entire day)

d) Be in *The Happy Place* (calm, happy, relaxed) (we will get to school, and we might skip brushing hair. Let's do what we can and better yet, what are we going to prepare for tomorrow morning so this isn't so challenging?)

2. Face to face with a certain ex-mother in law. I have the option to:
   a) Give the hairy eye-ball glare (temporary satisfaction only would be my guess)
   b) Ignore her (why start playing games now?!)
   c) Share false nice-ities (don't have the energy and goes against my value of being real)
   d) Be in *The Happy Place* (calm, relaxed and happy) (she is whom she is and I am who I am. For the few times in the rest of my children's lives that she will be in my presence, I will acknowledge her for who she is: A woman who loves my boys very much and wants the best for them, just like I do.)

3. When I have a list of 22 items to do in a day.
   a) Run and get them done (temporary satisfaction only and realization that I got sucked into a bad habit that I've stopped doing a while ago)
   b) Get stumped and frustrated (ruin my day with the burden of trying to fit all these things in, feel stressed about it and project it into everything else I do all day.
   c) Ignore it (but truthfully not ignore it because I don't have that power so the complete a combination of a) and b) and end up just as messed up!)
   d) Be in *The Happy Place* (calm, relaxed, and happy). The review list, prioritise based on need and urgency (as you now know as 'Must-ticks'). Ask others for assistance/support. Complete as

necessary. Then celebrate me doing it this way—this is still a HUGE thing for me.

The Happy Place is different for everyone. It can be a powerful perspective tool to assist you with finding out what a happy place is for yourself (what your wants are) and how you want to live (connecting to the values that are important to you).

I live out of this place about 80-85% of the time. Do I still have work to do—Yes. Yet I no longer evoke stress in others because of the stress I am carrying in myself. I celebrate staying connected to *The Happy Place*; it feels wonderful. I feel true to myself. Happier, more relaxed, enjoying my days, more connection with my kids and calm. And this is only the beginning.

So . . . you've already completed *The Happy Place exercise* a couple pages ago. Now you've read two experiences of it. Reread the questions you were asked. Explore your *Happy Place* deeper. Get more descriptive. Be there, feel it, touch it, picture it. Own it—it's yours and yours only. Lucky you.

25

THE CORE OF IT ALL

I need to share more with you about vulnerability. I think, relatively speaking, it's new to me. I'm still transitioning into it fully, and I'm going to do my hardest to hold on it.

What does "comfortable in your own skin" mean to you?

_____

_____

_____

_____

_____

_____

_____

_____

For me 'comfortable in my own skin' is like a calmness, even an aura that almost radiates around you, allowing you to be yourself fully, being unconcerned of other's judgements, almost unaware of others judgements because of your knowledge that theirs are only that . . . judgements. It's confidence, a sense of self, it's wholeheartedness, it's the ability to take risks, it's challenging myself on any fears I have, it's putting yourself out there and learning from the result of that, it's connectedness. It's what I want for my children. It's what I'm darn close in having for myself.

From my list above, what it all comes down to for me is one word. Vulnerability.

Vulnerability is a tough word for many people. Things that come to mind when you hear this word is "soft, wimpy, weak, inept". Yowwwch! Who wants to be that?!

Some people are taught early on in life to 'stay complete' is to be vulnerable. That both the act of feeling & sharing feelings, all feelings, is part of we are as humans. Many people are taught to not express or show vulnerability. It's like children being disciplined when they cry "Don't be a baby, suck it up", kids who are shy "Come out from behind my leg, you're not shy", or fear "Come on, you'll be fine, just go do it."

When I looked up vulnerability on line (thank you Online Encyclopedia) (19) here's what I found:

Vulnerability: the state of being vulnerable or exposed; susceptibility to injury or attack.

And look at all these 'feel good' (and so were clear, that was sarcasm) substitute word options that are available for vulnerability.

assailability, breakability, breakableness, brittleness, chink, crackability, crackableness, crispness, crumbliness, crushability, crushableness, delicacy, disqualification, exposure, extemporaneousness, fissility, flimsiness, fracturableness, fragility, frailty, frangibility, friability, heel of Achilles, improvisation, incapability, incompetence, lacerability, lack of preparation, liability, nonpreparation, nonpreparedness, openness, penetrability, planlessness, pregnability, soft spot, susceptibility, susceptivity, unfitness, unfittedness, unpreparedness, unqualification, unqualifiedness, unreadiness, unsuitability, unsuitableness, unsuitedness, vincibility, vulnerable point, weak link, weak point, weakness (20)

Again—not a usual arena that people say "yah, I want some of THAT!"

I've got mixed thoughts on the way Webster defines vulnerability. I don't think Master Webster has depicted vulnerability as a positive trait, yet instead as a negative one; one that may set you up for failure.

Did you notice that none of the examples I shared for what is said to children were about showing positive emotions? "Johnny, stop smiling so much, you're making others feel awkward." "Betsy, your pride is too clear regarding your effort on your school project, tone it down." Interesting.

So to recap:

Showing positive emotions = good to do

Showing the remaining range of feelings= don't do it.

My perspective of vulnerability is the reverse of this. Funny . . . for me being vulnerable means being authentic with your emotions. It means sharing what you really think, expressing emotions as you feel them, telling others what comes to mind when you see them, finding a balance between "thinking before you act" and jumping in with blinders on. It's being comfortable enough with yourself to do/say/act as you feel fit, without concern of other's judgement. It's consistently taking risks (big or small) with that attitude that this is what you do in life, simply to learn, to grow, to stay true to your being, to full connect with self. For me, vulnerability is the courage to lose.

Vulnerability takes courage. Massive courage. And I say massive courage because so many of us have been prodded through the years not to show & share vulnerabilities. So doing so seems so much more like a cliff jump because we're not use to the feelings that go with the sharing of the vulnerability. It's putting <u>you</u> out there. We were taught at such a young age how to act, behave, ask for things, follow rules, etc. Going against those set paradigms may feel awkward to you. Ask yourself this though—does it feel awkward because it's wrong or awkward because it's new? Because the first time I drove a car was a tad awkward (I failed my licence test twice) yet, I'm glad I persevered. Let's look at some other examples:

- In a past job I held, a colleague and now good friend of mine would pipe up in any meeting and simply say 'I don't get it. Explain it to me.' I had never seen this before. I had heard other people say things like "I must be stupid I'm not getting it—try me again" but never with the confidence Beth had when she asked.

If it were me (not getting it) I would continue to nod and plod my way through the meeting, and then ask someone later what was meant or try to piece it together on my own. *No exposing me I tell you!*

- Two friends of mine have each lost over 80 pounds.

- Math. Never a strong suit for me. I accept that. In a previous National Account Manager role I held I would call close friends and ask them for the formulas I needed to pull the sales numbers my Director asked me for. *Not good to not know something.*

- A friend of mine lost her baby girl at birth. She shared with me that it took her a really long time to realize that instead of allowing herself to feel the grief of losing her daughter, she was so desperate to move on and be able to find happiness again, that she was fighting the grief (vulnerability) and therefore, unable to move on. It wasn't until she truly let herself feel it as a whole, to be comfortable with the sadness that she truly began to be able to move ahead and be in a place where she could feel real happiness again. *"Can't go over it. Can't go under it. Can't go around it. Gotta go through it."*

- I took tap dancing lessons from age 6-17 years of age. After my first son was born, at age 32 I started dancing again. And it had nothing to do with me wearing a sunbeam consume and all to do with doing something I love. Who says you have to be 6 years old to tap dance? *Isn't tap dancing just for kids?*

- A client, that after dating his girlfriend for 12 weeks, (she left Canada to teach English in Japan) packed up and moved there after only 10 days. 8 years later, they are married and living in Canada with three children. *This is it—and I have to act on it.*

- A friend who was living in a beautiful tropical paradise; nice home, good job, good money, and a single parent. At the age of 46, she moved herself and her son to another country to follow her dream. *If I don't try, I'll never know.*

Vulnerability.

A willingness to ask for something you want. *"Will you go out with me?" "Will you show me how to work out so I can lose weight?"*

A willingness to try something new. *"I've never done this before, will you teach me?"* *"This scares the crap out of me yet, I'll try it"*

A willingness to be first. *"I love you."* *"I'll be first to jump"*

A willingness to take risks. *"If I don't try, I will always regret it."*

My last example; In a recent dating experience, I completely put myself out there. Like "wowie" out there. I shared openly and freely. I asked about anything that interest me and shared answers to whatever questions were asked. I did what came first to mind versus thinking 'no, that may be too much, he'll think I'm trying to _____.'. I enjoyed, I learned, I started to love. Then we broke up. And it REALLY hurt. This was my first heartbreak in a long time. Yet, I am filled with no regret. None. Why? Because I wouldn't do a thing differently. I was completely vulnerable in the relationship. I was completely real. The relationship showed me this was just the beginning of what I could have in a relationship and although painful at the time, a reminder to me of the self importance of being all or nothing to myself.

I'm a believer that to have all the good feelings stuff—happiness, joy, thrill, connection—you need to be able to feel all the tough feeling stuff at the same threshold—pain, anger, sadness, grief. You can't just have the good stuff; you need experience the full spectrum to keep your heart pumping and to be able reach the levels of WOW you deserve.

Brene Brown (great research speaker I had the opportunity to watch) (21) speaks of vulnerability being the birthplace of joy, love, peace, happiness. She suggests that when people fully embraced vulnerability it is both necessary (for their lives to be what and who they are) and that vulnerable makes them beautiful and allows them to live wholeheartedly.

I'm with Brene on this. The difference with Brene and I. Brene can prove this with research, me I prove it through life change.

QUESTIONS TO PONDER:

What's the biggest risk you've ever taken?

_____
_____
_____
_____
_____
_____
_____
_____

What did you gain by trying?

_____
_____
_____
_____
_____
_____
_____
_____

What did you lose by taking the risk?

_____
_____
_____
_____
_____
_____
_____

Define vulnerability in your own words:

_____
_____
_____
_____
_____
_____
_____
_____

What makes if positive for you?

_____
_____
_____
_____
_____
_____
_____

What makes it negative for you?

_____
_____
_____
_____
_____
_____
_____

What vulnerability (felt emotion) is currently holding you back in your life?

_____

_____

_____

_____

_____

_____

_____

_____

What currently makes you feel most vulnerable and you therefore hide/ guard it from others?

_____

_____

_____

_____

_____

_____

_____

_____

What are you losing because of it?

_____

_____

_____

_____

_____

_____

_____

What emotion do you want more of in your life?

_____
_____
_____
_____
_____
_____
_____
_____

What are you going to do starting today to make that happen?

_____
_____
_____
_____
_____
_____
_____
_____

What's one thing you need to stop doing today to allow you to share this emotion?

_____
_____
_____
_____
_____
_____
_____
_____

26

BECAUSE WE ALL HAVE A STORY

Ironically, I started writing *The Happy Place* with the primary subject being "who are you?" I explained my take on the experience of others introducing themselves and what they both share and don't share, leading us to the (hopefully) thought-provoking inquiry for yourself of who am I, really?

So this is it: My final chapter of my first book. As I've been writing this it's been interesting to me what people's responses have been about me writing a book. Some of those include:

- So what are you writing about?
- Wow, good for you, how exciting!
- Really, what's the topic?

My personal favourite was a girlfriend of mine who said, "Nance, what makes you the expert on this topic and why would people (buy and) read it." Loved her honesty, loved her curiosity, loved her *push* of me. I've thought about this a number of times in the last couple months. To date, my answer is 'I am living proof that by leading my life with my inside (my core values and beliefs) on the outside, the life journey is enriched for me, and anyone I touch. I believe my Intentional Communication life approach can be beneficial for anyone.'

I often share with coaching clients that we all have a story, yet oddly, lots of people refer to it as baggage, not a story (or a u-haul for that matter, that pulls and carries all our life baggage). Look at the difference of those perspectives. When most of us consider a story we think positive, happy ending, lots of character building, adventure, a little romance, good plot, quick pace, etc. When most of us think baggage, we tend to think more negatively; the hanging on of experiences we've had, not properly dealing with things of the past, hang-ups, character flaws, issues, etc. CRAZY how different the two are.

Which perspective do you share on this? Do you have a story or baggage?

I guess you could say we all have both. Depending on your opinion on it, you could say we have one, the other or both. Three years ago I would have voted that we all had (some) baggage. Now, my vote is different. Definitely different.

Worth noting in case I haven't been clear, in my opinion it is okay to have baggage. Here's the catch: are you a) hauling it around for the sake of hauling it or b) actively opening up the bag(s), sorting them, refolding, discarding a couple items, giving items back to others that were never yours to carry, etc. Heavy weight makes heavy lifting. On the other hand, reviewing your baggage content and sifting through it may provide learnings and insight. Sort your baggage and see what's in there for you.

My perspective on this life thing is that we are to be living it; living our choices, being fully present, connecting with our values, reaching our optimum, connecting our Life Dots. We can sway from that or stay in that; either way we will still continue to create our story. At one point in my life, probably through a combination of my own judgements, generalizations and response to past experiences among other things, I started following a story line. The 'what I thought the story was suppose to be' versus the creation of my own story. This took me off my own path of authenticity. This shifted me from being true to myself, from reaching for what I really wanted and striving for what I believe in. Then, in reflection one evening, taking stock at where I was in 'my story', I realised just how *off* I was from what was important to me. So I did a couple things:

1) I purposefully took back ownership and accountability for my own life
2) I sifted through some sludge to reconnect with my values and now lead by them

When I stray from those values, something ka-bonks me in the head and my gut does a rollercoaster loop. Then I get back to really <u>BE</u>ing in this life of mine.

It's a good feeling. Great feeling actually. This life is fully mine now.

Reviewing *The Happy Place* chapters today I got to thinking 'when my sons one day ask what their mom's life was all about what will be shared with them?'

They could be told: *Born and raised in Etobicoke, Ontario Canada. Had an older sister, mother and grandmother that she loved dearly. Was a facilitator and Coach and loved what she did. Was passionate about it. Was a jogger and in one of her races even won a car!*

Nothing listed above is false. All of these are important things about me. Thing I would want my cherished boys to know. Yet, you just finished reading this book. So you tell me, if you were me, what would you want my boys to hear? The story listed above, about my roles in life? Or the story about the values that kept me connected to the roles the made me tick in life.

We all have a story. What's yours? And better yet, what's still to be written?

The next chapter of your journey begins today. What's your story? Connect your dots.

xo

My name _____ *is and this is my story.*

_____

_____

_____

_____

_____

_____

_____

_____

_____

_____

_____

_____

_____

_____

_____

_____

_____

_____

_____

_____

_____

_____

_____

_____

_____

_____

_____

_____

_____

_____

_____

_____

_____

END NOTES

(1) The Coaches Training Institute, *"Co-Active coaching definition"*, http://www.thecoaches.com/why-coaches-training-institute/what-is-co-active (accessed 12 Nov. 2011).

(2) *Wikipedia, "Maslow's Hierarchy of Needs"*, en.wikipedia.org/wiki/Maslow's_hierarchy_of_needs (accessed 12 Sept. 2011).

(3) Henry Kimsey-House et al., *Co-Active Coaching Second Edition* (California: Davies-Black Publishing, 2007).

(4) Mo Willems, *Don't Let the Pigeon Drive the Bus!* (New York: Hyperion Books for Children, 2003).

(5) Gavin De Becker, *The Gift of Fear* (USA: Random House Publishing, 1999).

(6) Marlene and Bob Neufeld, *"Listening Filters"*, www.marleneandbob.com/listeningfilters/pdf based on the work of Drs. Gay & Kathlyn Hendricks, www.hendricks.com and on Non-violent communication (accessed 2 Oct. 2010).

(7) Water Outreach, *"Facilitation Skills—Listening Filters"*, http://wateroutreach.uwex.edu/education/filters.cfm (accessed 8 Feb. 2011).

(8) Geoff Farmsworth, *"The First Step in Skilful Communication"* http://vitalrelationships.com/the-first-step-in-skillful-communication/ (accessed 15 Feb. 2011).

(9) Henry Kimsey-House et al., *Co-Active Coaching Second Edition* (California: Davies-Black Publishing, 2007).

(10) Joan Hill, *Mastering Leadership.* Core Consulting Inc. www.coreconsultinginc.ca (accessed 2010-2011).

(11) Henry Kimsey-House et al., *Co-Active Coaching Second Edition* (California: Davies-Black Publishing, 2007).

(12) EMU Human Resources Service Centre Managing for Performance, *"How to set and write S.M.A.R.T. Objectives"*, http://www.hr.ecu.edu.au/mps/html/mps-smart.cfm (accessed 22 Dec. 2011).

(13) *Ally McBeal.* (Fox, 1997-2002; 20th Century Fox 2006 dvd).

(14) *Searchin' My Soul Tonight, Vonda Shepard.*, 1992.

(15) Andre Agassi, *Open* (New York: Vintage Books, 2009) 11.

(16) Tim Sanders, *Love is a Killer App.* (Crown Business, 2003).

(17) Naughty by Nature, *O.P.P.,* Anthem Inc. 1991.

(18) *Fun, in The Free Dictionary,* http://www.thefreedictionary.com/fun (accessed 25 Jan. 2013)

(19) *Vulnerable, in ENCYCLO Online Encyclopedia, http://www.encyclo. co.uk/define/vulnerability* (accessed 11 Jan. 2011).

(20) *Vulnerable,* in Merriam-Websters, http://www.merriam-webster.com/ thesaurus/vulnerable (accessed 11 Jan.2011).

(21) Ted X Talks, *"Brene Brown: The Power of Vulnerability"* http://www. ted.com/talks/brene_brown_on_vulnerability.html (accessed 27 Aug. 2011).

Appendix A

a) Sample template to capture your action plan in

	Desired Outcome	Measurable	Key Actions	Realistic	Timing
1	*In this area capture the development goal you want to develop*	*List here the "how" you'll know this has been achieved. i.e. evaluation, testing, exhibiting, presenting skills, mastery, etc*	*List the what needs to be done to get you to your end goal here.*	*Update progress on development goal here. If this doesn't reflect what was listed for the last two columns, adjust your plan to what's realisitic.*	*Identify a time line for each step*
2					
3					
4					

b) **Actual sample**

Let's say I wanted to run a half marathon. I could say "I want to run a half marathon" and you probably say something like "wow—good luck" yet, it would be unclear how I was going to get to that end goal.

Applying the SMART objective process, the different approach is:

I will train to run the Oakville Half Marathon September 7, 2012 with a goal time of 1hour 40 minutes and will prepare to do so by following the below training guide.

Clearly, the second statement is more believable for completion. Now there's an opportunity for you to give that to your own goals.

Week	4 INTERVAL DAYS				Long Run	Capture any required program tweaks here & total kms completed
	1	2	3	4		
	TUESDAYS	**THURSDAYS**	**FRIDAYS**	**SUNDAYS**		
July 13	Bike, weights & abs	Hill training (8) & 5km	sprints, arm weights & sit-ups, 7km speed run	10 km— regular run	10	
July 20	Bike, weights & abs	Hill training (8) 5km	sprints, arm weights & sit-ups, 7km speed run	10 with sprints	12	
July 27	Bike, weights & abs	Hill training (8) 5km	sprints, arm weights & sit-ups, 7km speed run	12 km— regular run	14	
Aug 3	Bike, weights & abs	Hill training (10) & 5km	7 km run, arm weights & sit-ups	14 km— regular run	16	
Aug 10	Bike, weights & abs	Hill training (12) & 5km	10 km run, arm weights & sit-ups	16 km— with sprints	18	

Aug 17	Elliptical, weights & abs	Hill training (14) & 5km	sprints, arm weights & sit-ups, 9km speed run	18 km— regular run	20	
Aug 24	Bike, weights & abs	Hill training (14)& 5km	7 km run, arm weights & sit-ups	20km— regular run	22	
Aug 31	Elliptical, weights & abs	Hill training (16) & 5km	5 km run, arm weights & sit-ups	18 km— with sprints	18	
Sept 7				**RACE DAY**	22	

About the Author

Nancy Milton is a University educated; CTI & ICF certified International Coach, Life Skills Speaker and Intentional Communication Facilitator. She was driven to write The Happy Place to reach more people than her practise can allow and continues to blog as she builds momentum for book two. Her company Life Dots works with both blue chip companies as well as targeted community groups and individuals keen to reach their life wants. An adventure enthusiast, community leader and tireless fundraiser Nancy stays connected to her happy place with beach walks and big bowls of peanut butter and chocolate ice cream.

Book questions, comments and typos can be sent to nancy@lifedots.ca or www.lifedots.ca

Follow Nancy's blog at http://www.lifedots.ca/blog.html

Facebook: facebook.com/LifeDotsCanada

Twitter: https://twitter.com/LifeDots

Linkedin: http://ca.linkedin.com/in/nancymiltonlifedots